The Trouble with
"Truth through Personality"

The Trouble with
"Truth through Personality"

Phillips Brooks, Incarnation, and the Evangelical Boundaries of Preaching

CHARLES W. FULLER

FOREWORD BY
HERSHAEL W. YORK

WIPF *&* STOCK · Eugene, Oregon

THE TROUBLE WITH "TRUTH THROUGH PERSONALITY"
Phillips Brooks, Incarnation, and the Evangelical Boundaries of Preaching

Wipf and Stock
A Division of Wipf and Stock Publishers
199 W. 8th Ave., Suite 3
Eugene, OR 97401
www.wipfandstock.com

ISBN: 978-1-60899-403-8

Manufactured in the U.S.A.

To Jessie,
my bride, lover, friend, and refiner;

to Kaylen and Ian,
my children, my joy, my heritage;

to a church of joyful believers,
who long for the pure milk of the Word;

and for a generation of evangelical pastors,
who desire to preach the Word faithfully.

"We dare not identify truth so closely with our own selfhood that we relativize it in our preaching to the point that the Word of God preached is a human word cut free from the written Word."

JOHN A. HUFFMAN JR.

Contents

Foreword

PREACHING IS PARADOX: a divine message voiced by an earthen vessel, speaking timeless truth in a specific moment from an ancient text to a contemporary world. To preach is to plumb the depths of that paradox with every sermon. The preacher needs boldness, but requires a great measure of humility. He should fear no reaction, yet be in tune with his audience. His prophetic voice must avoid no subject, though he is limited to the written text of Scripture.

Every preacher who repeatedly has dared to stand before a congregation, claiming to bring a word from God, has at times felt crushed by those contradictions. Trapped somewhere between audacity and fear, the preacher often may sense the internal fire of the Word quenched by the cold reality of a less-than-receptive church.

As a result, preachers have always struggled with the nature of the relationship between the external source of their preaching and their unique circumstances. The Bible itself highlights the connection, particularly through the Old Testament prophets. Jeremiah's rejection and imprisonment compounded the urgency of his warnings. Hosea's own betrayal bore witness to the love of a God who would take his people back in spite of their faithlessness and failure. The death of Ezekiel's wife, followed by his uncharacteristic lack of emotion, made the people ask, "What does this mean to *us*?" Whether in the pages of Scripture or a local church pulpit, the incidental blend of the message and the messenger is in fact essential and indissoluble.

Phillips Brooks's 1877 Beecher Lectures on Preaching became one of the most significant efforts ever to grapple with that crucial paradox. Just how can one uphold the distinctive nature of truth *and* the obvious importance of the human messenger? What makes the same message dull and lifeless in some contexts and vibrant and virile in others? How can one preacher engage the members of his congregation, holding them spellbound, while the same words emanating from another might seem tedious and tiresome?

In answer to this line of inquiry, Brooks proposed a definition of preaching that is as elegant and profound as it is succinct and memorable. Preaching, according to Brooks, is "truth through personality." His analysis took hold, acknowledging both sides of the preaching equation in the most concise formula imaginable. Had Brooks trademarked his phrase and lived to collect royalties, he might have been wealthy by the dawn of the twenty-first century. Hardly any book on preaching does not at least quote that line. Most borrow heavily from it in one form or another, and many authors have used it as a convenient delineation between what they believe are the two broadest categories for analysis.

Ironically, the very people who cite this line from Brooks often hold widely disparate views of preaching, the nature of what it is, and how it should be done. Narrative preachers, expositors, first-person preachers, roundtable preachers, and recent emergent church preachers quote Brooks authoritatively. Conservative, moderate, and liberal preachers alike enthusiastically appeal to Brooks's epigrammatic characterization. The divergence of views on preaching by its proponents alone would be enough to raise suspicion about its precise meaning but, until now, no one has bothered to ask the question and investigate exactly what Brooks intended when he first uttered the phrase in his lectures at Yale.

Charles W. Fuller's *The Trouble with "Truth through Personality"* is both overdue and groundbreaking. I confess that I had joined the chorus of homileticians who have paid homage to Brooks without bothering to question what he meant until I read this manuscript. I was more delighted than embarrassed, however, both by the company in which I found myself as well as by Fuller's penetrating insight. Fuller exposes the ease with which so many authors and preaching professors have cited Brooks without actually understanding his milieu or his meaning. Until this important work, no one realized that "truth through personality" has been the Rorschach test of homiletics, allowing each one who quotes it to see in it whatever he wants.

Through his thoughtful research and its eloquent presentation, Fuller painstakingly investigates Brooks's theology and philosophy of preaching, and demonstrates what Brooks meant so clearly that one can then decide intelligently whether or not one agrees with Brooks. That alone would be an important service to evangelical homiletics, but the genius of this work is that Fuller proposes a reconstruction of the "truth through personality" definition of preaching that redeems it from virtual meaninglessness and affords it a clear bibliocentric approach. Walking the tightrope anchored by truth on one end and personality on the other, Fuller offers the contemporary evangelical a line on which he can find balance and support.

Preaching can never be without paradox because it is inherently a supernatural act carried out by natural means. Frankly, Brooks's own definition lost sight of that very truth, while Fuller moves it to the forefront where it belongs.

Hershael W. York
The Southern Baptist Theological Seminary

Preface

CORRECT THINKING IS INDISPENSABLE to correct practice. I pen this preface just moments before leaving my office to venture to a local hospital for a visit with a man—a deacon in my congregation—who faces open-heart surgery. Before he submits his body to the surgeon for a critically important procedure, he will first want some assurance that the surgeon thinks rightly concerning the task. The surgeon indeed should have an intimate, impeccable understanding of the human cardiovascular system, the type of disease that threatens my friend's well-being, the various treatment options, the risks associated with each one, and the procedures required for the chosen course of action. Only by means of clear thinking through these categories will the physician acquire the necessary skills to perform the operation successfully. Experience remains vital—it is hoped that my friend will not be the doctor's first attempt at bypass surgery—but the effort will be futile and deadly without correct thinking based on correct knowledge.

I have written this book so that preachers might think correctly with regard to preaching. Evangelical Christians confess that preaching Christ is God's means of performing saving surgery on the human soul—a procedure with implications that are far more serious than an open-heart operation. The eternal destinies of human souls hang in the balance as the preacher stands to declare the grace and glory of the crucified and risen Christ. Therefore, preachers must think clearly of the task and understand it deeply to fulfill it faithfully.

I regret that charting out the evangelical boundaries for preaching requires a largely negative assessment of Phillips Brooks—a mammoth figure in the history of American preaching. The esteem Brooks received in his own day and the respect he still demands are not without due. In my study, I have found Brooks to be amicable, compassionate, and thoughtful, possessing a magnanimous vision for humanity and a genuine love for the individuals he encountered. His insistence on the value of the human soul and the importance of building character are themes largely missing from twenty-first-century American culture and, more lamentably, from some pulpits. His personal theological system and the preaching theory that stemmed from it are, however, fatally flawed. The extent to which his romantic, transcendental convictions compromise his evangelical roots must be highlighted, so that the dangers lurking in his concept of preaching may be exposed and avoided. The continuing popularity of Brooks's *Lectures on Preaching* among ministerial students, professional preachers, and academic homileticians underscores the need for careful and sustained analysis of his views.

I further regret that, in writing this volume, I have been critical of some highly regarded contemporary evangelical preachers. Men such as Bryan Chapell, Greg Heisler, Wayne McDill, Stephen Olford, Haddon Robinson, Jerry Vines, and Warren Wiersbe have shaped my own theology and practice of preaching. Their blunder in endorsing Brooks's definition of preaching constitutes just a minor error because, frankly, they do not mean what Brooks meant with the phrase "truth through personality." By quoting Brooks in a commending manner, though, they reveal a theological and historical blind spot. I hope that this volume sheds light on and provides sight into the unsighted mistake. Preventing further inaccuracies continues to be significant because, if Brooks's thoughts seep deeply into the minds of contemporary evangelicals, then faithful preaching and the gospel itself are in peril. Gladly, my pursuit of Brooks's faults results in redeeming the phrase "truth through personality" as a helpful axiom for thinking clearly with respect to preaching. Reconstructing the phrase with soundly evangelical doctrinal categories conveys what the aforementioned authors intend.

Acknowledgments

WHILE THIS VOLUME EMANATES from years of reading, research, and reflection, I could not have completed it without the support of others—such is the value of Christian community. My years of doctoral studies at The Southern Baptist Theological Seminary in Louisville, Kentucky, forced me to consider my presuppositions carefully and hone my principles precisely. Professor Hershael York, who graciously penned the foreword to this work and served as my doctoral supervisor, has done more than he knows to infuse my heart with a passion for preaching and to sear my mind with biblical principles for its pursuit. He is a consummate preacher, a faithful pastor, and an astute scholar. Buck Run Baptist Church, Baptists across Kentucky, the Southern Baptist Convention, and believers worldwide—particularly in Brazil—experience his influence greatly, and should be grateful. Professors Chad Brand, Theodore Cabal, and Robert Vogel likewise helped solidify my theological philosophical foundations for Christian preaching, and I am blessed to have studied under each one. The material supplied during seminars, the feedback offered by peers, and the guidance furnished by personal interaction made my experience in the doctoral program a meaningful and delightful journey.

Four churches deserve an appreciative mention. Liberty Baptist Church—in Madisonville, Kentucky—taught me the Scriptures from birth, and I came to personal faith in the Lord Jesus Christ through its witness. Pellville Baptist Church—in Pellville, Kentucky—loved me like a son and raised me in the ministry. While among the great gathering of believers in that tiny community, I saw firsthand the Lord's faithful response when his people obey his commands. Limestone Baptist Church—in Bedford, Indiana—gave me my initial opportunity to preach and teach on a weekly basis, and I feel as though I grew more by serving the members of that congregation than they benefited from my work. Bethany Baptist Church—in Louisville, Kentucky—has welcomed my ministry, embraced my family, provided for my needs, prayed for my efforts, enthusiastically encouraged me, and even granted me a study sabbatical to make this project possible. Marilyn Anderson, who is the Ministry Assistant at Bethany Baptist Church and the copyeditor for this volume, merits more thanks than I can give for her diligent labor.

The prayers and love of my family have been invaluable. I was granted the immense and irreplaceable providence of being raised in a faithful Christian home, and I hold my mother, Charlet; my father, Charles S.; and my brother, Chesley, in highest regards. Nothing, however, I might say here could possibly express my deep gratitude to my wife, Jessie. She is my lover, friend, partner, refiner, and supporter. To list the sacrifices that Jessie has made for enabling my work as pastor, student, professor, and author would require more volumes than I have the wherewithal to write. She remains a rock of mature, Christian stability—wonderfully mothering our two children, Kaylen and Ian; diligently serving our congregation; and wholeheartedly loving her husband. Proverbs 31:10 asks, "An excellent wife, who can find?" I do not know, but surely an excellent wife found me.

"Now to Him who is able to do far more abundantly all that we ask or think, according to the power that works within us, to Him be the glory in the church and in Christ Jesus to all generations forever and ever. Amen" (Eph 3:20).

Charles W. Fuller
Louisville, Kentucky

Introduction

A FRESH DISCUSSION OF Phillips Brooks's "truth through personality" preaching concept helps fill a gaping hole in contemporary discussions of the theology of preaching. Richard Lischer, in surveying the homiletical theories across the centuries, observes,

> The person of the preacher is a good example of a topic that was once of great importance to the medieval church but is now seldom discussed in homiletics. . . . Despite the new wave of interest in spirituality in the church today, one discerns no revival of the classical concern for the holiness of the preacher. The book on the preacher's holiness . . . has not been written. The recent discovery of "my story" as a major element in what is sometimes called autobiographical preaching is not a substitute for Christian character, without which the sermon is only words.[1]

Since the time of Lischer's observation, evangelical textbooks on preaching have given more attention to calling for personal holiness in the preacher, but still devote very little space to defining specifically the role of the preacher's personality in the event of preaching.[2] Typically, homileticians simply cite Brooks and then speak vaguely about an idea of "incarnational preaching," yet rarely does the reader discover any serious delineation of what such terms mean. Others have written more directly about the subject, but their works tend to slide completely into either rhetorical or hermeneutical discussion.[3] Additionally, as postmodernism seeps more deeply into the contemporary Christian mindset, those seeking to align Christianity with the movements of culture increasingly

---

1. Lischer, *Theories of Preaching*, 3.

2. Notice the very brief summaries that largely rely on Brooks in various textbooks. See Chapell, *Christ-Centered Preaching*, 36; Olford, *Anointed Expository Preaching*, 232–34; Robinson, *Biblical Preaching*, 25–27; Vines and Shaddix, *Power in the Pulpit*, 25–26.

3. See Hogan and Reid, *Connecting with the Congregation*; Thulin, *The "I" of the Sermon*; Cosgrove and Edgerton, *In Other Words*; Resner, *Preacher and Cross*.

employ the term "incarnational" in regard to preaching. David Teague contends that postmodern people respond best to preaching that is transparent, genuine, respectful, and "focused on God." For this reason, preachers should embrace an "incarnational" model, in which Christian proclamation becomes "preaching out of the encounter with God that we live out in our lives."[4]

Perhaps the term "incarnational" is simply a trendy way of affirming the old truth that preachers should practice what they preach. The persistent comparison, however, between *sui generis* events—like Christ's incarnation and Christian preaching—presents a substantial blur in the relationship between the preacher and the Word of God that, without clarification, tiptoes to the precipice of heresy. In response, evaluating the modern fountainhead of the problem—namely, Phillips Brooks's classic definition—seems in order. A full discussion, review, and reconstruction of "truth through personality" primarily furnish a clearer idea of how an incarnational motif applies to preaching, with its implications and limitations, and aids attempts to provide evangelical doctrinal underpinnings for a theology of the person of the preacher. Secondarily, the effort displays the ramifications of soteriology on homiletics.

This book assesses, from an evangelical perspective, Brooks's classic definition of preaching as "truth through personality" and, after pinpointing its substantial weaknesses, salvages the concept by reconstructing it with solidly evangelical doctrines. While Brooks's classic definition of preaching as "truth through personality" strikes a chord with most contemporary evangelicals, the way in which Brooks conceived his model actually presents significant deficiencies and dangers for evangelical preaching. Heavily influenced by romanticism—and based almost solely on an overextended, universalized, and thoroughly anthropocentric application of the incarnation of Jesus Christ—Brooks's idea, as his preaching demonstrates, descends into eloquent but anemic religious sentimentality and moralistic humanism. In addition, "truth through personality" in Brooks's scheme offers significant threats to a sound theology of preaching. The concept too closely associates the Word of God with the personality of the preacher, embraces a form of rhetorical *ēthos* that is antithetical to the gospel, and greatly mitigates the role of the text in sermon preparation and delivery.

---

4. Teague, "Incarnational Preaching," para. 4.

Salvaging the concept of "truth through personality" as an axiom for evangelical preaching, though, requires reconstructing the idea upon evangelical doctrines. Orthodox Protestant views of anthropology and soteriology must balance any implication that the incarnation of Jesus Christ has for preaching. Maintaining sound doctrines of sin and atonement serves to clarify the preacher's relation to the Word by implicating the preacher as a sinner saved by grace and a personal witness of a divine message, not as an unfettered incarnation of the Word of God. These same doctrines are controlling factors for the role of the preacher's personality in the event of preaching. The apostle Paul clearly made use of himself in his preaching and even employed rhetorical appeals that—at some level—can be placed in category with Aristotle's concept of *ēthos*, but his use of self was brought under the rubric of the cross and dictated by the gospel, the *logos* itself.[5] Rooted in a correct, balanced, evangelical theology, "truth through personality" can be recovered as a very useful tool in building an enduring definition of preaching.

PRELIMINARY CONSIDERATIONS

The term "evangelical" serves as the all-important modifier used to describe how this study queries, assesses, and reconstructs Brooks's concept of "truth through personality" as an axiom of Christian preaching. While evangelicalism has not been a homogeneous movement by any stretch, in this book the term "evangelical" refers to a particular theological tradition affirming mainly that the gospel is the good news that "by faith alone in Christ's death and resurrection alone may guilty sinners be forgiven of sin and be righteous before a holy God."[6] Other doctrines held by evangelicals include the authority of Scripture, the sovereignty of God, the Trinity, original sin, substitutionary atonement, bodily resurrection, and final judgment.[7] David W. Bebbington's quadrilateral definition of evangelicalism as conversionism, activism, biblicism, and crucicentrism offers a helpful paradigm for testing Brooks's core convictions.[8] Bebbington admits that evangelicalism has experienced signif-

5. See Resner, *Preacher and Cross.*

6. Mohler et al., "What Does It Mean to Be an Evangelical?" 4–9.

7. Ibid.

8. Bebbington, *Evangelicalism in Modern Britain,* 2–3; idem, "Evangelicalism in Its Settings," 366.

icant changes and shifts, but he nonetheless asserts that his quadrilateral definition represents the "common features that have lasted from the first half of the eighteenth century to the second half of the twentieth."[9] This work, therefore, seeks to pinpoint the theological and philosophical underpinnings of Brooks's definition; identify their strengths and weaknesses in view of orthodox evangelical doctrines; and recommend necessary corrections to maintain the concept in a consistent, evangelical manner. Chapter organization reflects this specific flow of thought.

Phillips Brooks in Academic Study

Much has been written about Phillips Brooks, and a voluminous multitude of his sermons, essays, and addresses have found their way into publication. Significant biographical works by Allen, Lawrence, and Raymond Albright amply document his life. A substantial amount of primary source material from Brooks, mostly in the forms of personal correspondence and otherwise unpublished material, appears in Allen's three volumes. At theological seminaries and universities alike, Brooks has been the topic of several doctoral dissertations focusing on his rhetorical theory, his pulpit effectiveness, his general approach to homiletics, his pastoral ministry, his role in ending slavery in the United States, and his concepts of morality and intellectual life. Harp rightly comments, however, that despite the attention Brooks has drawn during the years, he has "attracted comparatively little academic interest," and his theology has not "received much sustained scrutiny."[10] Just one doctoral dissertation, written by Alfred Benson Minyard at Boston University in 1957, endeavors to systematize Brooks's doctrinal convictions, and only Brastow and a few others have tried to trace his theological thought.[11] In Norman McLeod's 1960 doctoral dissertation at Union Theological Seminary, he suggests that his is the first genuinely critical study of Brooks,[12] and a serious critique of Brooks's place in the history of American Protestantism did not appear until Gillis Harp's book, *Brahmin Prophet*, was published in 2003.

---

9. Bebbington, *Evangelicalism in Modern Britain*, 2.

10. Harp, *Brahmin Prophet*, 2.

11. See Minyard, "Theology of Phillips Brooks"; Brastow, *Representative Modern Preachers*, 217–36; Politzer, "Theological Ideas," 157–69.

12. McLeod, "Levels of Relevance," 5–7.

Academic pursuit of Phillips Brooks presents a threefold problem. First, his immense popularity caused any biographical reflection on him to assume a "ponderously reverential" tone.[13] McLeod loathes Allen's extensive biography, criticizing its selectivity in material and referring to its sixteen hundred pages as an "unbroken tone of sheerest praise," which hangs "a screen between the reader and the man" and offers only a "figure of legend and myth."[14] Indeed, all three major Brooks biographies were penned by Episcopal admirers, reflecting a tendency for the denomination to serve itself with protective forms of biography.[15] Even two of the more recent biographical surveys, penned by David B. Chesebrough and John F. Woolverton, seemingly skew facts and events in Brooks's favor.[16] Only McLeod and Harp make genuine attempts at more objective assessments. Harp's work focuses broadly on the influences that shaped Brooks and his subsequent significance in Protestant and homiletical history, and McLeod's work concerns the extent to which Brooks diluted biblical truth in favor of cultural relevance.[17] In a sense, the present work builds upon Harp's keen insights, but focuses more narrowly on Brooks's definition of preaching.

Second, the persistent theological ambiguity of Brooks's sermons and lectures makes identifying his theological views an arduous task. Like F. W. Robertson, whom he greatly admired, Brooks often resisted making precise doctrinal deductions.[18] "When I am interesting, I am vague," Brooks once admitted to a friend. "When I am definite, I am dull."[19] For example, in one Good Friday sermon, Brooks says,

> Now what relation this death of Jesus may have borne to the nature and the plans of God, I hold it the most futile and irreverent

---

13. Harp, *Brahmin Prophet*, 2.

14. McLeod, "Levels of Relevance," 136–38.

15. Guelzo, "Ritualism, Romanism, and Rebellion," 553. The three major biographies of Brooks are Lawrence, *Life of Phillips Brooks*; Allen, *Life and Letters*; and Albright, *Focus on Infinity*.

16. Chesebrough, *Pulpit Eloquence*; Woolverton, *Education of Phillips Brooks*. Harp gives Woolverton's work a slightly better assessment. See Harp, "The Young Phillips Brooks," 652.

17. Harp, *Brahmin Prophet*, 3–4; McLeod, "Levels of Relevance," 1.

18. Robertson, *Sermons: Second Series*, 204; Wiersbe, "Preacher of Truth and Life," 16–17.

19. Brooks, quoted in Jones, *Royalty of the Pulpit*, 20.

of all investigations to inquire. I do not know, and I do not believe that any theology is so much wiser than my ignorance as to know, the sacred mysteries that passed in the courts of the Divine Existence when the miracle of Calvary was made perfect.[20]

Similarly, when approaching the topic of original sin, Brooks asserts,

Original sin means some sort of tendency or possibility of sinfulness. I take it to express nothing more than something vague and indefinite—it does not say what—something in man which makes it certain that as he grows up into manhood he shall grow up into transgression.[21]

Such vagueness has created a diversity of conclusions among those who have sought to identify Brooks's convictions, although many seek to retain Brooks among evangelicals.

Third, most intellectual historians dismiss Brooks quickly as a "superficial idealist."[22] Brooks read widely, but was not a scholar. "His mind was not profound," writes T. Harwood Pattison, "and he often illustrated his subject without explaining it."[23] When considered together, these factors likely account for the reality that his famous definition of preaching as "truth through personality" has been—to this point—embraced and quoted, but not adequately studied and evaluated.

Procedural Technique

Understanding Brooks correctly requires a substantial survey of his own work, with subsequent systemization and summary to clarify the philosophical thought, theological constructs, and homiletical theories that inform his definition of preaching as "truth through personality." Primary source material from Brooks's career—in the form of sermons and lectures, with particular attention given to his *Lectures on Preaching*—serves as the major basis for query. Selected sermons that deal pertinently with Brooks's convictions on the nature of truth, revelation, the incarnation of Christ, anthropology, soteriology, and homiletics receive the most attention. While I make no attempt to construct yet another biography of Brooks, certainly some biographical, academic,

---

20. Brooks, "Good Friday," 257.
21. Brooks, "Mystery of Iniquity," 6.
22. Ibid.; May, *Protestant Churches*, 64–67.
23. Pattison, *History of Christian Preaching*, 384.

and other reflective work helps in tracing his ideas and placing them in the context of his ministry and progressing maturity. Throughout this work, Brooks's convictions are compared to evangelical doctrines as expressed by major theologians, mostly ranging from the Reformation to the present. Points of consistency and strength merit due notation, but significant contrasts highlight the deficiencies of Brooks's "truth through personality" concept. Specific deficiencies are then examined to discover their roots and reveal their dangers for evangelical, expository preaching. Throughout the assessment, general observations of Brooks's sermon-preparation habits, exegetical method, and manner of delivery concretize his thoughts and illustrate the way in which his theology shaped his preaching. Finally, reconstructing a consistently evangelical concept of "truth through personality" for Christian preaching involves placing it within an evangelical framework, balancing the doctrine of incarnation with those of revelation and justification. In the end, the inquiry, evaluation, and reconstruction serve to establish foundations and boundaries for an evangelical concept of "truth through personality" as an axiom for Christian preaching and delineate specific guidelines for the preacher's conscious use of self in evangelical expository preaching.

1

"Truth through Personality": Legacy and Problem

URING HIS LYMAN BEECHER LECTURES ON PREACHING at Yale
University in 1877, Phillips Brooks stated:

> Preaching is the communication of truth by man to man. It has in
> it two essential elements, truth and personality. Neither of those
> can it spare and still be preaching. . . . [P]reaching is the bringing
> of truth through personality.[1]

Brooks's concept has been hailed as "perhaps the most famous definition
of preaching found anywhere in American homiletical literature."[2] The
enduring fame of Brooks's definition flows largely from the equally lasting renown of his preaching. While he served as the pastor of Boston's
Trinity Church and later as bishop over the Protestant Episcopal Diocese
of Massachusetts, Brooks's sermons left strong—almost mesmerizing—
impressions on listeners. In 1874, John Tulloch, Principal of St. Mary's
College in Aberdeen, visited Boston. After interacting with local elites
like Henry Wadsworth Longfellow, Ralph Waldo Emerson, and Oliver
Wendell Holmes, he attended a worship service to hear Brooks preach.
He immediately wrote to his wife:

> I have just heard the most remarkable sermon I have ever heard
> in my life . . . from Mr. Phillips Brooks. . . . I have never heard
> preaching like it, and you know how slow I am to praise preach-
> ers. So much thought and so much life combined; such a reach of
> mind, such a depth and insight of soul. I was electrified. I could
> have got up and shouted.[3]

---

1. Brooks, *Lectures*, 5.
2. Wiersbe, "Preacher of Truth and Life," 9.
3. Oliphant, *A Memoir*, 292.

Tulloch's sentiments represent the consensus response to Brooks of his contemporaries. Alexander V. G. Allen, Brooks's most thorough biographer, contends that newspapers across the nation displayed a "singular unanimity of utterance" concerning the public's high regard for Brooks, and suggests that a study of his impact on the public psyche would "in itself possess high value as a revelation of some reserved power in the Christian ministry, never so manifested before."[4] Allowing for Allen's exaggerative language, the facts of Brooks's ministry speak clearly enough. His preaching not only filled Trinity Church on Sundays, but throngs of Boston's businessmen and intelligentsia packed the building to hear his lunchtime sermons on weekdays.[5] When Brooks died in 1893, the city came to a standstill on the day of his funeral as thousands clogged the streets around Trinity Church, and nearly all businesses—including the stock exchange—suspended activities. Memorial services were held as far away as California and England. Within a week of his death, the effort to build a statue in his likeness brought in so much money that other memorial projects had to be started, and some donations were turned away.[6] The Reverend Brooks was so revered that some even suggested he was, more than any other man, "Christ incarnate."[7] On January 23, 1903, at a ceremony marking the tenth anniversary of his passing, Brooks's successor, William Lawrence, spoke no hyperbole by saying that the impact of Brooks

> passed over all denominational boundaries. Thousands outside his own church looked to him as their religious interpreter and pastor. . . . No one church, therefore, can claim him as exclusively hers. He belonged to the Christian world of the nineteenth century.[8]

With their colossal and far-reaching influence, Brooks's lectures at Yale were to many nothing less than the unveiling of a homiletical hero's secrets of success. When Brooks received the invitation to deliver

---

4. Allen, *Life and Letters*, 3:361. Allen's case is overstated, thereby displaying his bias toward Brooks, but his observations are not completely without merit. Allen's work has been sharply criticized for its hyperbolic praise of Brooks. See McLeod, "Levels of Relevance," 136, 138.

5. Hyde, "Rev. Phillips Brooks," 716–17.

6. McLeod, "Levels of Relevance," 133–35.

7. Thwing, "Power and Method," 178.

8. Lawrence, *A Study*, 41–43.

the Beecher lectures, he began pondering "the principles" by which he had "only half consciously been living and working for many years."[9] As the lectures came to pass, the secrets—or principles—became clear and could be summarized in one simple phrase: truth through personality. Expressed by a highly celebrated master of the pulpit, this grammatically economical, yet conceptually profound, definition of preaching moved quickly to the forefront of homiletics and was widely discussed throughout the opening decades of the twentieth century and beyond.[10] Even after the passing of more than a century, in a preface to a 1989 reprint of the *Lectures on Preaching*, Warren Wiersbe makes the audacious claim that "everything useful written on homiletics in America . . . is in one way or another a footnote to Phillips Brooks."[11]

"TRUTH THROUGH PERSONALITY" AND ITS LEGACY AMONG EVANGELICALS

Besides Brooks's immense ministerial popularity, another significant contributor to the remarkable durability of his concept of preaching arises from a particular convenience that it provides to evangelicals in their attempts to define preaching. Christian preaching involves a complex multiplicity of interrelated theological facets, rendering the event notoriously difficult to classify. For its ground, God himself ordains preaching as an ecclesiological function entrusted to the elders (1 Tim 3:2; 5:17), thereby making preaching "a gracious creation of God and a central part of His revealed will for the church."[12] Certainly, "preach the Word" (2 Tim 4:2) is the inescapable imperative for every local church and a distinguishing mark of the true church.[13] For its purpose, preaching plays an irreplaceable role in God's redemptive plan to bring sinners to salvation and subsequently to lead saints into sanctification.

9. Brooks, *Lectures*, 1.

10. Davis, "Quarter-Century," 137.

11. Wiersbe, "Preacher of Truth and Life," 7.

12. Mohler, "A Theology of Preaching," 13.

13. Calvin and Luther both ground the identity of the church in the preaching of the Word. Article seven of the Augsburg Confession defines the church as "the congregation of saints in which the gospel is rightly taught and the Sacraments rightly administered." Quoted from Schaff, *Creeds of Christendom*, 3:11–12. Calvin concurs, saying, "Wherever we see the Word of God purely preached and heard, and the sacraments administered according to Christ's institution, there, it is not to be doubted, a church of God exists." Calvin *Institutes* 4.1.9.

"We proclaim Him," writes the apostle Paul, "admonishing every man and teaching every man with all wisdom, so that we may present every man complete in Christ" (Col 1:28). Sidney Greidanus speaks for the majority when he says, "God uses . . . preaching to bring his salvation to people today, to build his church, to bring in his kingdom."[14] Moreover, few would argue against the maxim that

> God uses preaching to present His saints complete in Christ. How are Christians going to grow? How are they going to be matured? How is the process of Holy Spirit-directed sanctification going to be seen in them? It is going to occur by the preaching of the Word.[15]

For its mode, preaching, while not itself revelation, falls in line with the form of special revelation in that God communicates his Word by means of human agency. John Calvin sums up the matter nicely in claiming that "because [God] does not dwell among us in visible presence, we have said that he uses the ministry of men to declare openly his will to us by mouth, as sort of delegated work, not by transferring to them his right and honor, but only that through their mouths he may do his own work—just as a workman uses a tool to do his work."[16] Preaching cannot, therefore, be replicated or characterized in purely secular or non-Christian terms. Preaching is *sui generis* in the church—a category all its own.[17] John A. Broadus affirms, "Preaching is characteristic of Christianity. No false religion has ever provided for the regular and frequent assembling of the masses of men, to hear religious instruction and exhortation."[18]

The inimitable nature of Christian preaching causes many of the best evangelical homileticians to stop short of pinning down a concrete definition for it. Albert Mohler, in composing a homiletical theology, describes—but does not specifically define—preaching, saying, "The act of preaching brings forth a combination of exposition, testimony, exhortation, and teaching. Still, preaching cannot be reduced to any of these, or even to the sum total of its individual parts combined."[19] Haddon

---

14. Greidanus, *Modern Preacher and Ancient Text*, 9.

15. Mohler, "Primacy of Preaching," 28–29.

16. Calvin *Institutes* 4.3.1.

17. Dargan, *History of Preaching*, 2:14; Mohler, "Theology of Preaching," 13.

18. Broadus, *Treatise*, 17.

19. Mohler, "Theology of Preaching," 14.

Robinson displays a similar ambiguity when he admits, "Preaching is a living process involving God, the preacher, and the congregation, and no definition can pretend to capture that dynamic."[20] D. Martyn Lloyd-Jones, celebrated for his exactitude, offers only a brief definition by asserting, "Preaching is theology coming through a man who is on fire." Even this succinct demarcation comes only after his confession that preaching "is certainly not a matter of rules and regulations. . . . Preaching is something one recognises when one hears it. So the best we can do is say certain things about it."[21] Other evangelicals, however, make strides in offering more precision. J. I. Packer defines preaching as "the event of God bringing to an audience a Bible-based, Christ-related, life-impacting message of instruction and direction from Himself through the words of a spokesperson."[22] Similarly, Jerry Vines attests that preaching is the "oral communication of biblical truth by the Holy Spirit through a human personality to a given audience with the intent of enabling a positive response."[23]

Whether indistinct or exact, all these attempts to define preaching find a common ground in the formidable and nearly legendary definition offered by Brooks. Even in the opening decade of the twenty-first century, several of the more widely read evangelical textbooks on preaching still give "truth through personality" a tacit if not wholesale endorsement, including those authored by Bryan Chapell, Greg Heisler, Wayne McDill, Stephen Olford, Robinson, John Stott, and Vines.[24] Brooks's concept of preaching still "rings true" for them because it "reflects biblical principle as well as common sense."[25] On the muddled matter of the nature of preaching, therefore, it seems that "truth through personality" provides a ready refuge for evangelicals. The idea resounds with God's command that his truth—revealed through human agency—continue to be communicated through human agency, and it certainly envelops

---

20. Robinson, *Biblical Preaching*, 21.

21. Lloyd-Jones, *Preaching and Preachers*, 81, 97.

22. Packer, "Authority in Preaching," 199.

23. Vines and Shaddix, *Power in the Pulpit*, 27.

24. Chapell, *Christ-Centered Preaching*, 36; Heisler, *Spirit-Led Preaching*, 97–98; McDill, *Moment of Truth*, 23; Olford, *Anointed Expository Preaching*, 233; Robinson, *Biblical Preaching*, 25; Stott, *Between Two Worlds*, 266; Vines and Shaddix, *Power in the Pulpit*, 25.

25. McDill, *Moment of Truth*, 24; Chapell, *Christ-Centered Preaching*, 36.

the conviction that the person-to-person confrontation of preaching ("teaching" and "admonishing" in Col 1:28) represents a means by which preaching accomplishes its redemptive objective.

"TRUTH THROUGH PERSONALITY" AND ITS PROBLEM FOR EVANGELICALS

While "truth through personality" as a general statement fits nicely into most evangelical preaching models, Gillis Harp notes in his book, *Brahmin Prophet*, that Brooks's thoughts on preaching actually represent a radical departure from the textual, doctrinal preaching passed down from prior evangelical Prostestants. According to Harp, Brooks's definition came as the fruit of a homiletical shift largely facilitated by a "softening of the dogmatic structure of evangelical Protestantism to the point that the quickening of the religious sentiment was widely held to be a better aim for the preacher than the inculcation of a fixed body of doctrine."[26] In other words, the idealism and romanticism of the Gilded Age combined to pave a smooth and palatable path away from objective, methodological, and dogmatic Christianity toward a more subjective, experiential, and doctrinally ambiguous form of the faith. The sum result for his pulpit was that

> the ministry of the word became inextricably bound up in Brooks's system with the personality of the preacher. Such an approach served to augment the evangelical cult of pulpit celebrity as it shifted away from the traditional emphasis on a body of defined propositional truth to be communicated. In this way, a Romanticized Christianity switched the primary focus from an external message . . . toward the subjective character of the messenger appealing to the religious sentiment of its auditors.[27]

By mitigating the component of external authority and maximizing the component of personal experience, Brooks took only one factor of Christian preaching and made it central: namely, the personality of the preacher.[28] Brooks, in his lectures, goes as far as to maintain that the preacher's personality, fully engaged, is the key to effective preaching, and that preaching itself is a revelation of the preacher's personality. He claims,

26. Buell, "The Unitarian Movement," 167.

27. Harp, *Brahmin Prophet*, 117.

28. Ibid.

The truth must come really through the person, not merely over his lips, not merely into his understanding and out through his pen. It must come through his character, his affections, his whole intellectual and moral being. It must come genuinely through him. I think that, granting equal intelligence and study, here is the great difference which we feel between two preachers of the Word. The Gospel has come over one of them and reaches us tinged and flavored with his superficial characteristics, belittled with his littleness. The Gospel has come through the other, and we receive it impressed and winged with all the earnestness and strength that there is in him. . . .

[A] man's best sermon is the best utterance of his life. It embodies and declares him. If it is really his, it tells more of him than his casual intercourse with his friends, or even the revelations of his domestic life. If it is really God's message through him, it brings him out in a way that no other experience of his life has power to do.[29]

Furthermore, because God's revelation to man primarily concerns revelation of himself and his personality more than it is a revelation of abstract or objective facts, any discussion of truth must reach the level of personality.[30] God is intensely personal, and the center of his personality is his will, so the truth that comes from him is directed toward the personalities and wills of people, his highest creations.[31]

Temporally speaking, one of the factors that ushered in Brooks's emphasis on personality and helped effect the weakening of Protestant theology in general is the intellectual challenge presented to Christianity as the Enlightenment descended from academia to the wider culture. Brooks preached during a time when the creedal foundations of the Christian faith appeared to crumble under attacks from Darwin's theory of evolution and German higher biblical criticism. Parishioners, feeling as though they had no reason to remain, exited the pews and entered new circles of thought that seemed more ready to deal with scientific developments, such as Spiritualism, Christian Science, and the New Thought.[32] Into this situation, Brooks became a "symbol of certainty in an age of doubt" by embodying a broad Christianity with the same calm

29. Brooks, *Lectures*, 8, 135.
30. Brastow, *Representative Modern Preachers*, 227, 229–30; Lawrence, *A Study*, 34.
31. Brastow, *Representative Modern Preachers*, 229–30.
32. McLeod, "Preaching of Phillips Brooks," 51.

confidence that these new circles exuded, thereby making the Christian religion believable again.[33] In one sermon, Brooks states,

> When He sees you and me trembling for fear lest such and such a theory may gather so much evidence that we cannot reject it, but will have to own it to be true, it seems to me that I can almost hear Him say, "My children, if it be true, do you not want to believe it? I have known it all along. By coming to the truth you come to me, who have held the truth in my bosom—nay, by whom the truth is true. Do not be frightened. I cannot be taken by surprise."[34]

He was "a good symbol—handsome, eloquent, romantically solitary, apparently so confident and full of faith, and untroubled by, though not unaware of, winds and currents that were leaving others in doubt and uncertainty,"[35] and thus "hundreds of people who felt themselves sinking into unbelief turned to him with the desperation of drowning men."[36]

Brooks's very personable approach, while in some sense a pragmatic response to the intellectual challenges of his time, was not without a theological foundation. Biographers and theologians alike consistently identify the incarnation of Christ as the very center of his doctrine and homiletic.[37] Allen asserts that the incarnation "became . . . the ground principle of his theology and of his life. . . . Over the mystery of the Incarnation Phillips Brooks was perpetually brooding, till it became to him what the doctrine of the 'Divine Sovereignty' had been to his Puritan ancestors."[38] Indeed, the incarnation was for Brooks what "knit the universe, God, and his creation into living unity,"[39] and hence gave preaching its highest paradigm. "There is no real leadership of people for a preacher," according to him, "except that which comes as the leadership of the Incarnation came."[40]

On the doctrinal level, Brooks's formulation of the incarnation was generally orthodox, in that he affirmed in Nicene fashion that Christ

---

33. Ibid., 56; see also Britton, "The Breadth of Orthodoxy," 144–62.

34. McLeod, "Preaching of Phillips Brooks," 59.

35. Ibid., 56–57.

36. Lawrence, *Phillips Brooks,* 85.

37. Brastow, *Representative Modern Preachers,* 232; White, "Preaching of Phillips Brooks," 70, 76; Wiersbe, "Preacher of Truth and Life," 16.

38. Allen, *Life and Letters,* 2:517–19.

39. Lawrence, *A Study,* 13.

40. Brooks, *Lectures,* 85.

was of the same essence as the Father, although he likely struggled with the two-nature distinction of Chalcedon.[41] Yet, as the "great Christian humanist" who "bent all his energies to the task of interpreting and ennobling human existence,"[42] Brooks applied the doctrine in a decidedly anthropocentric manner, using it in service of what was for him an even greater core truth and the very reason for preaching: the value of the human soul.[43] For Brooks, the incarnation displays a real affinity between God and man and proves that man is, by nature, a child of God.[44] Francis Ensley nicely captures the approach when he claims that Brooks

> regarded Christ's Incarnation as a specification of a universal principle that holds in all life. What he found in Jesus Christ he generalized. If the Incarnation portrays the actual humanity of God . . . it equally proclaims the potential divinity of man. If Jesus Christ is a revelation of what God is, he is also a sign of what man may become. . . . The Incarnation is at heart a doctrine about human potentiality, a confirmation of human hopes.[45]

In Brooks's own words, "Christ was what man had felt in his soul that he might be. Christ did what man's heart had always told him that it was in his humanity to do."[46]

Brooks's anthropological application of the incarnation wielded massive ramifications with respect to his soteriological views. While he did not explicitly deny the substitutionary atonement of Christ and at times he sounded quite evangelical in his views of justification,[47] a substantial amount of ambivalence on the nature of salvation appears in his lectures.[48] On balance, he seemed to locate redemption in humanity's

41. Ensley, "Phillips Brooks and the Incarnation," 352, 357; Allen, *Life and Letters,* 2:841.

42. Brastow, *Representative Modern Preachers,* 195–97. Brastow calls Brooks a "Christian humanist" in the sense that Brooks purported a lofty sense of humanity's worth, but maintained evangelical terminology in his anthropology. Wiersbe asserts, "In these beliefs, Brooks was certainly influenced by Horace Bushnell's *Christian Nurture.*" Wiersbe, "Preacher of Truth and Life," 20.

43. Brooks, *Lectures,* 255–56.

44. As opposed to the natural man being at enmity with God. Lawrence, *A Study,* 38–39; Allen, *Life and Letters,* 2:521.

45. Ensley, "Phillips Brooks and the Incarnation," 352–53.

46. Brooks, *Visions and Tasks,* 282.

47. White, "Preaching of Phillips Brooks," 88–90. See also Brooks, *Purpose and Use of Comfort,* 37–56.

48. Brooks, *Lectures,* 32–33.

innate ability to follow the pattern revealed in the incarnation. Christ's incarnation was for Brooks the uniting of wills, and salvation now occurs to the extent that incarnation—the uniting of wills—recurs.[49] In this way, salvation becomes less about the imputation of righteousness and more about the realization and actualization of righteousness already present. In a sermon titled "The Nearness of God," Brooks intimately connects the incarnation to salvation and final glorification, saying,

> Christ was not a God coming out of absence. He was the ever-present God, revealing how near He always was.
>
> And so of the new life of Christ in man. It is not something strange and foreign, brought from far away. It is the deepest possibility of man, revealed and made actual. When you stand at last complete in Christ, it is not some rare adornments which He has lent from His Divinity to clothe your humanity with. Those graces are the signs of your humanity. They are the flower of your human life, drawn out into luxuriance by the sunlight of the divine Love. You take them as your own, and wear them as the angels wear their wings.[50]

Although Lewis Brastow rightly notes the general vagueness of Brooks's theological expression, he aptly captures Brooks's basic soteriological thought in asserting,

> The atonement . . . must be conceived from the point of view of the incarnation. It is not, therefore, a transaction between a Christ and a God who stand outside of humanity, but who are revealed in and are identified with humanity, and the efficaciousness of the atonement is not in the sufferings of Christ, but in the obedience of His holy will. The reconciliation of God and man is not a forensic transaction dealing with ideal relations, but an actual participation of man in the righteousness of God. . . .
>
> The New Testament representation that man becomes a child of God by identification with Christ is based upon the already existing fact that he is such by nature. If he were not God's child by nature, he could never become His child by grace. Christianity does not create, but only declares, the fact, and furnishes the requisite provision for its realization. In coming to Christ we come to ourselves, as in coming to us, Christ "came to his own." Sin on its negative side is a failure to realize one's sonship with God; on its positive side, it is refusal to accept and actualize the fact. . . . Regeneration, conversion, sanctification, are the beginning and the completion

---

49. Brooks, *Visions and Tasks*, 291.
50. Brooks, *Seeking Life*, 56.

of the process by which one comes to the recognition of one's self
as a child of God, and lives agreeably to the fact.[51]

For Brooks, humanity is neither irrevocably good nor hopelessly de-
praved. Rather, humanity is the magnificent, infinitely valuable crown
jewel of God's creation, endowed with the ability to overcome the plague
of sin by following the perfect example set forth in the incarnation.
Consequently, the ultimate test of religion is whether or not it can "make
men better men."[52] Truth, flowing from the fount of the revelation of
God's personality in the incarnation and centered in His will, must be
infused into the personalities of people to build character. Preaching, as
a means to this end, serves to "translate speculative truth into personal
character and to relate it clearly and practically to daily life,"[53] and so
must be defined fundamentally as "truth through personality."

As any definition of preaching rests upon the theological convictions and constructions of its author,[54] the theological roots of Brooks's
concept of "truth through personality" should cause more discomfort
among evangelicals than has been expressed and spark more reflection
than has been pursued. Undoubtedly, "truth through personality" can
be filled with and sustained by evangelical convictions but, by blindly
citing Brooks and inserting his concept into more conservative models
of preaching, evangelicals run the risk of sanctioning that which they
would otherwise deny—namely, that preaching is merely an aid in the
effort to attain salvation through character-building. In order to employ
"truth through personality" in support of preaching models that affirm
an orthodox Protestant soteriology and focus heavily on biblical exposition, the concept needs to be comprehensively assessed and then reconstructed upon a more consistently evangelical foundation.

---

51. Brastow, *Representative Modern Preachers*, 232–33.

52. Brooks, *Essays and Addresses*, 545.

53. Albright, *Focus on Infinity*, 162.

54. The preaching textbooks by Chapell, McDill, Olford, Robinson, Stott, and Vines
all contain substantial sections about the theological underpinnings of preaching. For a
good statement on the connection between theology and homiletics, see Craddock, *As
One without Authority*, 3, 52–53.

2

The Rise of Romanticism

A N ASSESSMENT OF Phillips Brooks's definition of preaching is more
an analytical than it is a biographical endeavor—more about
Brooks's concept than about Brooks himself. The purpose of this chapter
is not, therefore, providing yet another extensive survey of his life and
work, even though the present task deems some biographical material
necessary. Neither is the goal of this chapter simply identifying again
the major influences in Brooks's thought, although these principal influences must be delineated. Rather, this chapter aims to set Brooks rightly
in his context by tracing the way in which certain biographical, philosophical, and theological factors form the roots of Brooks's definition of
preaching. Because of the rise of romanticism in the nineteenth century
and its concomitant rise in Brooks's thought, theology, and homiletical
theory, he emerges as a figure influenced much more by romanticism
than by historic evangelicalism.

ROMANTICISM IN NINETEENTH-CENTURY
EVANGELICALISM

William G. McLoughlin insightfully casts nineteenth-century evangelicalism as a period of great ideological fluctuation, during which
undercurrent shifts in philosophy caused sweeping changes in theology.[1] In the early part of the century, Reformed theologians effectively
used major tenets of Scottish Common Sense realism to combat deism,
mostly by pointing out consistencies between moral laws derived from
experience and those contained in the Bible.[2] Not long after, however,
the champions of the Second Great Awakening—especially Charles

1. McLoughlin, "Introduction," 1.
2. Ibid., 2–4.

G. Finney—challenged many of the premises of Calvinism, and a distinctly Arminian concept of God's relationship with man supplanted the Calvinistic concept that had to that time "dominated American thought."[3] By midcentury, the doctrinal distinctions between Calvinism and Arminianism faded to the point that denominations were divided simply as "evangelical" and "unevangelical."[4] McLoughlin, furthermore, purports that the era's idea of evangelicalism consisted of nothing more than the simple doctrines found in Lyman Beecher's 1823 sermon, "The Faith Once Delivered to the Saints": the Trinity, human freedom, atonement, and justification by faith.[5]

As Arminian evangelicalism celebrated the freedom of the individual in the midst of *laissez-faire* capitalism and Jacksonian democracy, an increasingly romantic strain of philosophy entered the American picture, owing much to "subtle infiltrations of post-Kantian idealism."[6] Romanticism was not a certified school of philosophy, but rather a "movement that affected all areas of life."[7] Beginning with Jean-Jacques Rousseau in France and Johann Herder in Germany, and including thinkers such as Freidrich Schlegel and Johann Schiller, romanticism started mostly as a rebellion against the naturalistic and empiricist limitations imposed by the Enlightenment. Borrowing a platonic metaphysic from Kantian idealism, romanticism reasserted the power of intuition and feeling, arguing that these subjective means provide access to ultimate realities that Enlightenment methodologies can never contemplate.[8] On the one hand, romanticism became something of an ally to Christianity during a period in which the Enlightenment threatened to reduce all reality to the natural and observable.[9] By separating faith from the realm of reason, romanticism reopened the religious doorway that the Enlightenment nearly closed. On the other hand, romanticism presented a real danger to Christianity in that its subjective "longing

3. Ibid., 4–5.

4. Baird, *Religion in America*, 287–88.

5. McLoughlin, "Introduction," 6; Beecher, *Faith Once Delivered*, 3–5. Notably, Beecher simply separates the "Evangelical System" from the "Liberal System" without reference to Calvinist or Arminian differences.

6. McLoughlin, "Introduction," 14. The precise relationship between romanticism and post-Kantian idealism proves difficult to portray due to similarities, interrelatedness, and somewhat simultaneous development.

7. Hicks, *Journey So Far*, 341.

8. Wilkins and Padgett, *Faith & Reason*, 24–25.

9. Copleston, *Modern Philosophy*, 147–48. See also Muirhead, *Platonic Tradition*.

for the infinite" tends to cast both nature and history as expressions of the divine mind and emphasize God's immanence to the point of bordering on pantheism. Such monistic continuity between the divine and the natural resulted in an extremely elevated view of humanity. David Friedrich Strauss came to consider Christ's incarnation as mythological, but symbolic of the deeper truth of the unity between the human and the divine, saying, "Humanity is the union of the two natures—God become man, the infinite manifesting itself in the finite, and the finite spirit remembering its infinitude."[10]

The chief nexus between romanticism and American Christianity in the nineteenth century occurs in writings of Samuel Taylor Coleridge, particularly in his *Aids to Reflection*. To protect Christian belief against critical methods, Coleridge reinterpreted Christianity "along the experiential directions offered by Romantic philosophy."[11] Coleridge, based in part on Kant's split between the phenomenal and the noumenal, distinguished between the "understanding" and the "reason." In Coleridge's thought, "understanding" refers to the passive human faculty that perceives the sensory world, and "reason" refers to a higher means of grasping spiritual truths that are beyond the reach of sensory experience.[12] Reason comprises both "the will and the moral aspect of human personality" and provides a more immediate knowledge of God.[13] McLoughlin summarizes:

> Since ultimate truth or divine truth is invisible, insubstantial, and ethereal then God must have given man some more certain way of ascertaining it than by mere reasoning from sense experience or common sense. . . . God had implanted in man an inner consciousness of intuitive sense of the divine which, properly aroused and alert, was able to perceive supernatural truth directly. The Reason was the power by which man received his real knowledge of the moral law emanating through Nature from the core of the universe. The experience of directly perceiving God in Nature through the inner eye of the soul awakened such intimations of immortality and sublimity as to be in themselves the highest form of spiritual communion between God and man. From such experiences man learned more about . . . true holiness than he could ever learn from most intricate speculations and deductions of Scottish metaphysics.[14]

10. Strauss, *Life of Jesus*, 780.

11. Wilkins and Padgett, *Faith & Reason*, 39–40.

12. Coleridge, *Aids to Reflection*, 194–95.

13. Copleston, *Modern Philosophy*, 152; Wilkins and Padgett, *Faith & Reason*, 44.

14. McLoughlin, "Introduction," 15.

In Coleridge's thought, "Whenever understanding touches spiritual reality, it inevitably corrupts it."[15]

Employing his scheme in support of Christianity, Coleridge believed that this higher search for unity with God by means of "reason" brings the awareness of disunity that Christianity then resolves. The proof of Christianity, though, lies not externally in an authority like Scripture, but rather internally in the individual. "The truth revealed through Christ has evidence in itself," Coleridge asserts, "and the proof of its divine authority [is] in its fitness to our nature and needs;—the clearness and cogency of this proof being proportionate to the degree of self-knowledge in each individual hearer."[16] Scripture, therefore, must be freed from claims of external authority and read from an internally experiential perspective. In this way, Coleridge largely accepted higher biblical criticism, but still found value in the Scriptures. "In the Bible," he states, "there is more that *finds* me than I have experienced in all other books put together; that the words of the Bible find me at greater depths of my being; and that whatever finds me brings with it an irresistible evidence of its having proceeded from the Holy Spirit."[17] For Coleridge, the law of conscience always maintained veto power over the "Canons of discursive Reasoning."[18]

In addition to realigning the authority of Scripture, Coleridge's system presented more revisions to traditional evangelicalism, including the refusal of typical intellectual proofs for Christianity, the rejection of total depravity, and the extreme loathing of systematized doctrines.[19] Although evangelicals were not ready to take Coleridge's model into full transcendentalism, the way in which his thought insulated Christianity from skepticism and absorbed the advance of biblical criticism found great appeal among some of the most prominent Christian thinkers of the time.[20] Horace Bushnell, who has been called the "most eminent American theologian between Edwards and Walter Rauschenbusch,"

---

15. Hicks, *Journey So Far*, 351.

16. Coleridge, *Confessions*, 86–87.

17. Ibid., 47.

18. Coleridge, *Aids to Reflection*, 155–56.

19. Ibid., 133; Hicks, *Journey So Far*, 351.

20. Sanders, *Coleridge and the Broad Church Movement*, 14; Wilkins and Padgett, *Faith & Reason*, 48–49; Harp, *Brahmin Prophet*, 151–52.

was powerfully affected by Coleridge.[21] Bushnell not only contended that truth is "not of the natural understanding," but also carried forward Coleridge's agenda by calling for an end to dogmatism, reducing the Bible to mere poetry, affirming that one could be nurtured as a Christian without a sudden and emotional conversion, proposing a moral influence theory of the atonement, and ultimately seeking to recast the Christian faith in wholly figurative language.[22] In regard to Phillips Brooks's denomination, the strongest link between Coleridge and the Episcopal Church can be found in Frederick Denison Maurice's *Theological Essays*, published in 1853.[23] A controversial figure, Maurice openly confessed his dependence on Coleridge and taught a heightened anthropology, saying that "man, as man, is the child of God. He does not need to become a child of God, he needs only to recognize that he already is such."[24]

The general effect of this romanticized Christianity on evangelicalism was a move from cognitive doctrines to a religion of the heart, rendering a form of the faith that was "too amorphous to be threatened by Darwin or the higher critics."[25] Indeed, romanticism provided the very avenue through which Christianity came to terms with the new challenges presented by Darwinism and biblical criticism. Viewing the Bible as poetry or literature conveniently mitigated the threat of criticism, and the romantic view of the progress of humanity seemed sufficient to support some "vague idea" of the evolutionary process.[26] McLoughlin notes that in this new, romanticized evangelicalism, the major emphases fell upon the emotions, the "personality of Jesus," and conversion through transfusing "Jesus Christ into your whole life."[27] The ministry of Henry Ward Beecher presents a microcosm of this shift. While claiming to be an evangelical Calvinist, Beecher nonetheless declared himself to be a

21. McLoughlin, "Introduction," 14.

22. Bushnell, *God in Christ*, 96; idem, *Christian Nurture*, 35–36; McLoughlin, "Introduction," 16; Harp, *Brahmin Prophet*, 25–26.

23. Harp, *Brahmin Prophet*, 152.

24. Maurice, *Kingdom of Christ*, 1:xv; Hutchinson, *Modernist Impulse*, 81.

25. McLoughlin, "Introduction," 23. Machen argues that the sole root of liberalism is naturalism. He appears to overlook, however, the way that romanticism enabled the amalgamation of Christianity and modernism. Machen, *Christianity and Liberalism*, 2.

26. McLoughlin, "Introduction," 22; Hankins, *American Evangelicals*, 23–26.

27. McLoughlin, "Introduction," 14, 20.

"cordial Christian evolutionist," appealed to aesthetic sensitivities in his preaching, and even said, "I apprehend that more men have been converted by the simple presentation of Christ as a Person than by the presentation of the Atonement as a doctrine."[28]

Some, of course, rejected this romantic turn. Charles Hodge, for example, championed the old Reformed doctrines at Princeton and labored to defend substitutionary atonement from the moral influence theory proposed by Bushnell.[29] Among Episcopalians, Charles P. McIlvaine and Stephen H. Tyng were creed dogmatists who held a very high view of Scripture, stressed substitutionary atonement as the central theme of Christian preaching, and pressed "home the truth with a tone of assurance that rests upon an external basis of authority."[30] Others, particularly D. L. Moody, adopted a moderate approach. He maintained the more conservative focus on atonement, regeneration, and conversion—while at the same time downplaying theological controversy to preach a simple, heartfelt gospel.[31] Regardless of these responses, however, the influence of romanticism—together with the general optimism of the nineteenth century—was pervasive enough that it allowed the term "evangelical" to be applied quite broadly. By the closing years of the century, "evangelicalism" often included wholesale romantics, those associated with the New Theology, and many who were actually more akin to what Lyman Beecher once called the "Liberal System."[32]

ROMANTICISM IN THE MINISTRY OF PHILLIPS BROOKS

A brief review of Brooks's life and ministry reveals an embodiment of the nineteenth-century swing toward a liberal, romantic form of the Christian faith. On December 13, 1835, William Gray Brooks and his wife, the former Mary Ann Phillips, welcomed into the world their second son, Phillips Brooks. Lewis Brastow's observation that Brooks was "the consummate flower of nine generations of cultured Puritan stock" is partially correct, if tainted in color.[33] Brooks's mother was raised in an

28. Lloyd, *Life of Henry Ward Beecher*, 151; McLoughlin, "Introduction," 20–22.

29. Hodge, *Anthropology*, 566–73.

30. McIlvaine, *Work of Preaching Christ*, 11, 35; Tyng, *Record of the Life*, 376–77; Brastow, *Modern Pulpit*, 207.

31. Gundry, *Love Them In*, 64–67.

32. Beecher, *Faith Once Delivered*, 5.

33. Brastow, *Representative Modern Preachers*, 195.

orthodox Trinitarian Congregational family. Her father, John Phillips, was one of the founders of Andover Theological Seminary and a defender of the "unimpaired . . . Puritan theological heritage."[34] Mrs. Brooks wielded powerful spiritual influence on her family, making Bible reading and prayer consistent household practices.[35] Four of her sons entered the ministry, and her frequent letters provided them with many theological pointers.[36] Brooks's father, William Gray Brooks, while a descendant of the famous Puritan John Cotton, grew up in a middle-class family with only a meager interest in education and religion.[37] In fact, William Gray Brooks was a Unitarian and, when he married Mary Ann Phillips in 1833, they continued to attend a Unitarian congregation until she could endure it no longer. In 1839, at her insistence, the family rented a pew at St. Paul's Episcopal Church in Boston, following a trend of dissatisfied Unitarians who sidestepped the Congregationalist schisms and became Episcopalians.[38] Interestingly, while Mrs. Brooks quickly became a member of St. Paul's, William Gray was not confirmed until May 30, 1847, at age 42 and after a significant personal struggle.[39]

Phillips Brooks grew up at St. Paul's under the preaching of Alexander H. Vinton, a pietistic systematic Calvinist, who emphasized emotional conversion.[40] Brooks always held Vinton in high regard, but certain aspects of Vinton's message irked Brooks, particularly in regard to Vinton's traditional evangelical perspective concerning humanity and wealth. When he was twenty years old, Brooks thus responded to one of Vinton's sermons:

> It is almost time for some men to learn that their incessant railing at Earthly riches & power & learning are doing far more harm than good. That men are really convinced on reasonable grounds that these things are good, worthy objects of ambition & endeavor, and that if they have higher & worthier advantages to offer their way to recommend them must not be to decry & deprecate what little good man already possesses. Such men may thank merely

34. Allen, *Life and Letters*, 1:27.

35. Harp, *Brahmin Prophet*, 14.

36. Ibid.; Wiersbe, "Preacher of Truth and Life," 10.

37. Harp, *Brahmin Prophet*, 14.

38. Allen, *Life and Letters*, 1:42–43; Harp, *Brahmin Prophet*, 14–15.

39. Allen, *Life and Letters*, 1:44.

40. *Dictionary of American Biography*, s.v. "Vinton, Alexander Hamilton."

the weakness of their cause & of themselves that their Efforts are not productive of more serious effects. Once convince men that wealth, power, & learning are mean & despicable & wrong & you have crowned inefficiency & ignorance, brutality & stupidity as the monarchs of our race forever.[41]

At Vinton's funeral in 1881, Brooks acknowledged Vinton's influence in his life, but also remarked, "Many of us who listened to Dr. Vinton thirty years ago have seen truth differently now from the way in which he showed it to us then."[42]

Phillips Brooks attended Boston Latin School and then graduated from Harvard College in 1851, ranking third in his class. While at Harvard, Brooks read insatiably, consuming voluminous works of Elizabethan poetry, eighteenth-century essayists, and particularly contemporary romantic authors. He found himself immersed in Alfred Tennyson's *In Memoriam* and became enraptured by Thomas Carlyle's heroic ideal, as displayed in his thesis on the Hugenot Paul Rabaut.[43] No one knows the extent to which these romantic works affected Brooks's religious thought at the time.[44] Allen points out, however, that a "scrutiny of his college essays reveals no tendency to dwell upon the subject of religion."[45]

After graduating from Harvard, Brooks accepted a teaching post at Boston Latin School, from which he resigned in less than six months, apparently falling prey to his own youthfulness and somewhat bashful demeanor.[46] His failure at teaching thrust Brooks into a sort of crisis that eventually led him toward Christian ministry. In the midst of Brooks's personal struggle, Vinton asked to see him for counsel, but Brooks chose instead to seek first the advice of James Walker, president at Harvard.[47] Only after Walker steered him toward ministry did Brooks seek Vinton's consent. Vinton approved and, in addition to suggesting Virginia Theological Seminary, he reminded Brooks that it was "customary to have received confirmation before becoming a candidate for

41. Brooks, quoted in Harp, *Brahmin Prophet*, 20.

42. Brooks, *Alexander Hamilton Vinton*, 13.

43. Harp, *Brahmin Prophet*, 21; Albright, *Focus on Infinity*, 24–29.

44. Allen, *Life and Letters*, 1:87.

45. Ibid., 1:90.

46. Albright, *Focus on Infinity*, 29–31; Allen, *Life and Letters*, 1:100–121.

47. Allen, *Life and Letters*, 1:121–22.

orders" and that "conversion was generally regarded as prerequisite for confirmation."[48] Brooks replied to this that he "did not know what conversion meant."[49] Raymond W. Albright reports that, in subsequent days, Brooks came to a "commitment . . . so complete that no other experience was ever able to reduce it to second place in his life," but Albright seems to be creating an impression of conversion without firm evidence.[50] John Woolverton confesses forthrightly that Brooks "never had a conversion experience."[51] Gillis Harp observes, "That the son of Mary Ann Phillips and a long-time parishioner of St. Paul's claimed not to understand the meaning of conversion suggested that some sort of internal rebellion against his evangelical upbringing had occurred at college."[52] Indeed, even Alexander Allen states that Brooks "had not been consciously reached by the religious teaching at St. Paul's, and to a certain extent was in revolt against it."[53]

Brooks's years at Virginia Theological Seminary (1856–59)—a low-church, conservative Episcopal school—were not easy ones, nor was he contented. He disliked the Southern culture, academic sloth, and dogmatic Calvinism taught in the classroom.[54] His perception of an anti-intellectual atmosphere led him to say, "I am living my common life here, surrounded with minds as dull & hearts as dead, & ears as deaf & tongues as dumb as my own."[55] Near the end of his first academic year, Brooks sought to leave Virginia for Andover Theological Seminary—a more innovative institution—but his father consulted Vinton, who

---

48. Ibid., 1:141–42.

49. Ibid., 1:142.

50. Albright, *Focus on Infinity*, 34. Allen refers to Brooks's commitment to ministry as a "ripening within him the consciousness that he was called by God"; and Brooks himself speaks of his decision as submission to a "larger motive," namely, "the sending of God." In regard to his conversion, Allen asserts that it came by a "process" typical in the nineteenth century. Allen, *Life and Letters*, 1:147, 266.

51. Woolverton, *Education of Phillips Brooks*, 50.

52. Harp, *Brahmin Prophet*, 22.

53. Allen, *Life and Letters*, 1:121.

54. Harp, *Brahmin Prophet*, 29–34. Brooks did, though, find friendship with William Sparrow, a faculty member at Virginia Seminary. Sparrow held an Arminian view of election and had a distaste for doctrinal wrangling. Woolverton, *Education of Phillips Brooks*, 74.

55. Brooks, quoted in Harp, *Brahmin Prophet*, 30.

predictably discouraged the move.[56] His dissatisfaction with Virginia Seminary, though, inspired him toward a more personal course of study. His notebooks from these years indicate that the works of Beecher, Bushnell, Coleridge, Johann Wolfgang Goethe, Maurice, Tennyson, and William Wordsworth filled his reading—an "amalgam of liberal Romantic Evangelicalism and literary Romanticism."[57] Allen reports that "no books in Brooks's library show signs of harder usage than Bushnell's *Sermons for the New Life*, and Maurice's *Theological Essays*."[58] Later, in 1864, his mother warned him against reading Bushnell's sermons, saying that they "tear the view of Christ's vicarious suffering all to pieces."[59] Like his college essays, Brooks's private writings in his seminary years yield "very few" references to the cross, "almost no" references to conversion, and "almost nothing" from the eighteenth-century evangelicals.[60] He dedicated only "cursory attention to Richard Hooker . . . and none at all . . . to the reformers of the sixteenth century."[61]

As Brooks inhaled romantic influences, he began to exhale evangelical doctrine. He openly rejected Calvinism and moved further away from major tenets of traditional evangelicalism, such as total depravity.[62] Brooks grew increasingly impatient with doctrinal systems altogether and, referring to the doctrines learned at Virginia Seminary, he observed, "We cannot but fear that very many of them are very far indeed from the truth."[63] His journal records, "I don't believe as this my neighbor does."[64] His frustrations with Virginia Seminary additionally prompted the opportunity for social development. Brooks expressed interest in a young lady named Jenny Fairfax in early 1857. He saw her frequently and spoke of her highly, but the relationship evidently ended abruptly in 1858.

56. Ibid., 31; Allen, *Life and Letters*, 1:168; Albright, *Focus on Infinity*, 38.

57. Harp, *Brahmin Prophet*, 28, 32–33.

58. Allen, *Phillips Brooks*, 67.

59. Woolverton, *Education of Phillips Brooks*, 15.

60. Harp, *Brahmin Prophet*, 36.

61. Woolverton, *Education of Phillips Brooks*, 90.

62. Harp, *Brahmin Prophet*, 33–34. Brooks says in a letter to a friend, "The Calvinist part, I emphatically reject." Allen, *Life and Letters*, 1:169.

63. Brooks, quoted in Allen, *Life and Letters*, 1:303–4.

64. Brooks, quoted in Harp, *Brahmin Prophet*, 35.

Brooks cited only "discord" and "distrust" as reasons.[65] He never again established a serious relationship with a woman and never married.

The day after graduating from Virginia Seminary on July 1, 1859, Brooks was ordained as a deacon. He moved to Philadelphia to pastor the Church of the Advent the very next month. He was ordained to the priesthood in 1860 and, on November 18, 1861, Brooks resigned his position at the Church of the Advent to become rector at Holy Trinity Church, also in Philadelphia. During the Civil War years, he became a champion for the Union's cause, an ally to abolitionists, and later an advocate for the rights of former slaves.[66] His forthright commitment to the Union was in "debt to Romanticism with its accent on following one's conscience," and his view of the war as the working out of Christ's kingdom was "a preview of the immanentism of his mature theology."[67] Romantic influences indeed inundated Brooks's thoughts toward Abraham Lincoln. Brooks identified Lincoln as a hero who fit Carlyle's ideal, and he even compared Lincoln's death—as exemplary and moral—to that of Jesus Christ.[68] In his Easter sermon on April 16, 1865, Brooks referred to the "correspondence between the day of the death of our martyred President and the day on which our Lord was crucified":

> If there has been any high heroism in the world, and any triumph over evil and iniquity, it has been only a faint repetition of that great work which the Perfect Man did when He triumphed once for all over sin, in behalf of His redeemed world. If there has been any man setting himself earnestly against iniquity as he found it at his especial time and place, it has been only a rebound from that courage with which Christ set himself against the wickedness that was in the world at his time. And if it so be that another Pontius Pilate, as weak as he, is made the agent of an iniquity as deep as that which brought the suffering Saviour to His death, and comes up and strikes at another man pure and good and true to some high object, shall we not say the day is fit? . . . And may we not derive example and inspiration from this new martyrdom and look forward to the resurrection promised out of it?[69]

65. Chesebrough, *Pulpit Eloquence*, 26; Woolverton, *Education of Phillips Brooks*, 60.

66. Harp, *Brahmin Prophet*, 48–56; Wiersbe, "Preacher of Truth and Life," 13; Albright, *Focus on Infinity*, 76–121.

67. Harp, *Brahmin Prophet*, 47.

68. Ibid., 56–57.

69. Brooks, quoted in Allen, *Life and Letters*, 2:11.

The romantic themes of progress, heroism, and immanence became increasingly evident in Brooks's ministry throughout these Civil War years.

Interestingly, during Brooks's Philadelphia years, he found a place within the Episcopal evangelical party—a group that retained the traditional doctrines. He supported the efforts of the Evangelical Education Society and even accepted an appointment to the new Philadelphia Divinity School faculty, although his vestry at Holy Trinity quickly convinced him to remain at the church instead.[70] Largely due to his popularity—and their need for a young leader—these Episcopal evangelicals greatly desired to claim Brooks as their own, but his resistance to theological systems and skepticism of precise doctrinal formulas caused some uneasiness. One colleague wondered whether Brooks's "so-called transcendental mind, with a rather thin coating of Evangelical theology . . . would square itself with the average Philadelphia layman's standard."[71] Allen notes that the "older men must even then have recognized some difference in the presentation of the truth as they held it," and records a very telling letter from a parishioner accusing Brooks of moralistic preaching that "borders on unsoundness."[72] Only later in Boston, however, did he more openly move away from these evangelical associations.

In 1869, Brooks accepted a call from Boston's Trinity Church and left Philadelphia for the "old-money elite" culture in which he was raised.[73] Within a year, Brooks encountered a significant confrontation with the evangelical party as the Evangelical Education Society tried to set higher, more strict doctrinal standards for the ordinands it sponsored. Brooks promptly resigned from the board and soon publicly distanced himself from the evangelical party.[74] In a eulogy that he delivered for the stalwart evangelical Bishop Manton Eastburn, Brooks seemed to declare the death of the old doctrines as well as the bishop, saying, "They were great truths."[75] Although Brooks maintained cordiality with several Episcopal evangelicals like Stephen H. Tyng and Charles Edward Cheney, and

70. Chesebrough, *Pulpit Eloquence*, 46–47; Harp, *Brahmin Prophet*, 72–73.

71. Newton, *Yesterday with the Fathers*, 24.

72. Allen, *Life and Letters*, 1:388, 2:123.

73. Harp, *Brahmin Prophet*, 11.

74. Ibid., 74–78. Harp rightly points out that most of Brooks's biographers have largely downplayed and nearly ignored this controversy.

75. Brooks, quoted in Allen, *Life and Letters*, 2:76.

enjoyed widespread appeal among traditional evangelicals, he became more and more identified with the Broad Church movement—a liberal wing among Episcopalians.[76] By means of some personal correspondence, Brooks gladly endorsed the Broad Church as "the party of the future" and, as older evangelicals died off, Brooks delightedly quoted what one of them said: "I am disposed to regard the prospects of our Church brighter now than they have ever been in my day."[77] The Boston Clerical club, which he founded, was "a microcosm of the larger Broad Church movement" and served as Brooks's "immediate intellectual circle" in the 1870s and 1880s.[78]

Brooks's popularity soared in Boston, and his influence stretched beyond theological and denominational lines, mostly because of his preaching. His sermons were imaginative, energetic, personal, pastoral, and persuasive.[79] They were distinct from the abstract, doctrinal sermons that many traditional evangelicals delivered. Brooks spoke less about certain truths of God and more as though he were speaking from God.[80] He was neither rigidly expository nor generally topical. He typically selected a grand theme, alluded to a biblical passage (often a single verse), and then launched into a dramatic argument with fluidity and grace.[81] In 1877, his growing celebrity earned him an invitation from Yale Divinity School to present the annual Lyman Beecher Lectureship on Preaching, in which he offered his now-famous definition of preaching as "truth through personality." It seems that this event marks a "distinct epoch," and perhaps the "real apex," of his career.[82] Brooks revealed in these lectures his ambivalence concerning the aim and mode of salvation and tiptoed around the implications of his claim that preachers should "seize the divine side of all humanity."[83] Brooks returned to Yale in 1878 to deliver two additional lectures and, in that same year, he published his first

76. Harp, *Brahmin Prophet*, 89–96, 156–59. The Broad Church movement refers loosely to a type of liberalism that arose among Episcopalians in the nineteenth century, which held that the "English church was, by the very conditions of its being, not High or Low, but Broad." Sanders, *Coleridge and the Broad Church Movement*, 7–8.

77. Brooks, quoted in Allen, *Life and Letters*, 2:207.

78. Harp, *Brahmin Prophet*, 157.

79. Turnbull, *From the Close of the Nineteenth Century*, 112–13.

80. Ibid., 112.

81. Ibid., 113; Harp, *Brahmin Prophet*, 122.

82. Albright, *Focus on Infinity*, 187.

83. Brooks, *Lectures*, 32–33, 47–49.

volume of sermons, *The Purpose and Use of Comfort*. In 1879, Brooks gave The Bohlen Lectures at Philadelphia Divinity School—later published as *The Influence of Jesus*—in which he combined an incarnational motif with Carlyle's heroic ideal to present Jesus' heroism in terms of morality, sociality, emotionality, and intellectuality.[84]

Throughout the 1880s, Brooks traveled extensively and spoke abroad. Even while wrestling with exhaustion, he rejected offers from Harvard and the University of Pennsylvania to assume less demanding academic posts, and even declined an opportunity to become the assistant bishop of the diocese of Pennsylvania.[85] In 1887, Trinity Church arranged for him to conduct a series of Sunday-evening meetings at Faneuil Hall, so that the poorer people on Boston's north side could hear the famed preacher.[86] During this decade, Brooks delivered several important lectures in which he more boldly revealed his thought. In a lecture called "Authority and Conscience," delivered in 1884 to the Ninth Congress of the Protestant Episcopal Church in Detroit, he undermined biblical infallibility and ecclesial authority in favor of the primacy of the individual conscience.[87] Speaking to the Cambridge Clericus Club in 1890, Brooks presented a very broad vision of orthodoxy, asserting the romantic notion that truth is "more moral than doctrinal, more personal than abstract."[88]

When Benjamin Paddock—Bishop of Massachusetts—died on March 9, 1891, Brooks quickly became the leading candidate to replace him. Brooks somewhat reluctantly accepted the nomination and was elected April 29, 1891. Traditional evangelicals and High Churchmen alike voiced their opposition, citing misgivings about his orthodoxy, ecclesial views, and baptism.[89] Brooks refused to respond to the charges. Brooks was confirmed in June, and—in October—he was consecrated in Trinity Church before a sizable crowd that included the governor of Massachusetts, the mayor of Boston, the president of Harvard, and four hundred clergymen.[90] The intense work of the episcopate, however, had a draining effect on Brooks, so that his health deteriorated. On Tuesday,

---

84. Brooks, *Influence of Jesus*; Allen, *Life and Letters*, 2:335–37.

85. Chesebrough, *Pulpit Eloquence*, 100–106.

86. Ibid., 107.

87. Brooks, "Authority and Conscience," 105–17.

88. Brooks, "Orthodoxy," 183–87.

89. Chesebrough, *Pulpit Eloquence*, 115.

90. Ibid., 117.

January 17, 1893, he took a cold and sore throat. Although a physician's visit on Thursday provided hope that the condition was not serious, Brooks was much worse by Sunday. He died—perhaps from diphtheria—on Monday, January 23.[91]

ROMANTICISM IN THE THEOLOGY OF PHILLIPS BROOKS

Alfred Minyard may be correct when he surmises that Brooks "broke further from the old Evangelical theology than he was usually prepared emotionally to recognize," but break he did.[92] While Brooks employed traditional evangelical terms—even using such words as "heresy" and "orthodoxy" in his essays, and terms like "conversion" in his sermons— his theology was shaped deeply by romantic notions, particularly those of Coleridge. Allen observes,

> [H]e lingered over Coleridge's poetry. What Coleridge had done for others he was doing now for him, emancipating from the false or worn-out logic of customary system, revealing the deeper meaning of the articles of the Christian faith, enlarging the conception of religion, restoring to reason its true place in the broken harmony between faith and knowledge. . . . Into this teaching Phillips Brooks was entering, and throughout his career rejoiced in the manifold riches it brought him.[93]

The influence of Romanticism on Brooks stretched all the way from his concept of truth to his thoughts on eternity, but a simple comparison utilizing David Bebbington's quadilateral sufficiently proves the extent to which romanticism pulled Brooks away from traditional evangelicalism. Keeping Brooks in his nineteenth-century context, the following sections compare Brooks's convictions to those of traditional evangelicals within his own time period.

Biblicism

Biblicism is a "particular regard for the Bible," according to Bebbington, and he claims that there is "agreement among Evangelicals of all generations that the Bible is inspired by God."[94] Charles McIlvaine set the

---

91. Ibid., 119.

92. Minyard, "Theology of Phillips Brooks," 25.

93. Allen, *Life and Letters*, 1:227–28.

94. Bebbington, *Evangelicalism in Modern Britain*, 3, 13.

traditional evangelical standard among Episcopalians in Brooks's day, explaining,

> God's Word is not merely *contained* in the Scriptures *somewhere*, but in the Scriptures *everywhere*; not merely that by his Inspiration *parts* of Scripture were given, leaving us to say what parts; but that all that belongs to holy Scripture was so given. This is Plenary Inspiration, in full sense of the words, as opposed to partial.[95]

In sharp contrast, Brooks assumed a position that followed Coleridge's experiential component and included Bushnell's approach to the Bible as human literature. For Brooks, Scripture is a human document; its only peculiar revelational quality comes insofar that it is a "noble story told by noble men," and speaks "not through passive trumpets, but through living history and acting characters."[96] In sermons and classes, Brooks displayed increasing favor toward biblical criticism and conveyed his belief that the Bible is merely the record of revelation. In a Wednesday-evening lecture at Boston's Trinity Church, he states,

> So to men God may declare Himself through manhood. Books may record that, but their real value is in *what they record*. . . . Thus Christ is the true Revelation of God, and the Bible gets its value from being the description of Christ. The *story* of a revelation, more properly than a revelation itself. And so its various parts differ with the quality of what they have to tell of. So the Revelation lies behind the Bible, and the Bible is to the Revelation like the sunshine to the sun. . . .
>
> And now, how did these writers write? The old theories of verbal and plenary inspiration. But without them look at the real state of the case. A solemn and dear person to be written about. A watching world. A deep sense of responsibility. A mind quickened by sympathy with his mind. All these together seem to make a power of accuracy and faithfulness which is all we could desire. . . .
>
> Does it involve unerring accuracy? Answer, "No."[97]

In one sermon delivered in 1887, Brooks again appears very comfortable with higher criticism and even announces the end of verbal inspiration, saying,

---

95. McIlvaine, quoted in Chorley, *Men and Movements*, 309.

96. Brooks, quoted in Allen, *Life and Letters*, 2:352.

97. Ibid., 3:94–95.

> To very many Christian men to-day the Bible stands no longer
> surrounded by that kind of supernatural authority which estab-
> lishes the truth of every statement in its pages. It has come to
> seem to many men what it really is, a gathering of many wonder-
> ful books from many times,—the time and authorship of some
> of them being doubtful,—which have been brought together
> because of their common character and their common bearing
> on one great religious process which runs through the history of
> man—the revelation of the Eternal Father to mankind in Jesus
> Christ. Clearly enough, such knowledge of the nature of the Bible
> must set the mind free for a treatment of it and a study of its
> contents such as has not always been possible. . . . The world will
> never go back again to the old ideas of verbal inspiration.[98]

Indeed, in some personal correspondence with one of his brothers,
Brooks endorses criticism so readily that he speaks harshly of the

> obstinate dishonesty of men who refuse to recognize any of the
> new light which has been thrown upon the Bible, and go on re-
> peating assertions about it, which, if there be any such thing as
> proof, have been thoroughly and repeatedly disproved. These are
> the men on whom the church in the future must look upon with
> reproach and almost with contempt.[99]

Brooks viewed the Bible not as a literal, verbal revelation from God to
man—as historic evangelicalism had affirmed—but rather as a window
into revelation and as an invitation to experience revelation—a decidedly romantic approach. In sum, Brooks asserted, "If the true revelation
of God is in Christ, the Bible is not properly a revelation, but the History
of a Revelation. This is not only a Fact but a necessity, for a Person cannot
be revealed in a Book, but must find revelation, if at all, in a Person."[100]

Crucicentrism

Bebbington defines crucicentrism as "a stress on the sacrifice of Christ
on the cross," and contends that the standard evangelical view holds that
"Christ died as a substitute for sinful mankind."[101] Charles Hodge, the
conservative evangelical stalwart, maintained substitutionary atonement
against all the competing theories in the nineteenth century, particularly

---

98. Ibid., 3:87.

99. Ibid., 2:420.

100. Ibid., 2:477.

101. Bebbington, *Evangelicalism in Modern Britain*, 3, 15.

against the moral influence theory of Coleridge and Bushnell. In the second volume of his classic *Systematic Theology,* he describes the doctrine plainly, asserting,

> According to this doctrine the work of Christ is a real satisfaction, of infinite inherent merit, to the vindicatory justice of God; so that He saves people by doing for them, and in their stead, what they were unable to do for themselves, satisfying the demands of the law in their behalf, and bearing its penalty in their stead; whereby they are reconciled to God.[102]

Brooks departed from this historic evangelical position and espoused a moral influence theory similar to that of Bushnell. Although Brooks often claimed ambivalence regarding the nature of the atonement, his preaching subtly revealed a moralistic take on its effect.

Two of Brooks's sermons furnish examples of his atonement formulations, which are repeated throughout his preaching. In a sermon titled "Good Friday," he initially states, "Now what relation this death of Jesus may have borne to the nature and the plans of God, I hold it the most futile and irreverent of all investigations to inquire," but then continues to say that "it seems clear that all we have to do with the death of Jesus is its aspect toward, its influence upon, humanity."[103] Brooks explains that Christ's death set forth a new truth: the forgiveness of sins. Humanity is painfully aware of its sin and the fact that sin bears consequences, and God the Father is the character of the Deity who executes justice and demands punishment. Jesus Christ, though, is the other character of the Deity who provides forgiveness.[104] Christ always existed for this purpose, but this objective could not "have its full effect until men knew of it."[105] When Christ came, "He wrote it out in blood," according to Brooks:

> He has hung it up where I must see it. He has laboriously translated it into human life, that I may not mistake it. And then, when He can do no more, when the truth that has been true forever has been thus fearfully announced, the work is over, and crying, "It is finished," the Saviour closes His eyes and drops His head and dies.
>
> Oh, what a finishing that was! . . . The long yearning to let men know what a love waited for them in the heart of God was satisfied.[106]

102. Hodge, *Anthropology,* 563.

103. Brooks, "Good Friday," 257–58.

104. Ibid., 262.

105. Ibid., 263–64.

106. Ibid., 265.

In other words, Jesus' death satisfied not God's justice, but his longing to declare a message of forgiveness. Forgiveness "is laid upon the heart with all the pathetic appeal of suffering," Brooks states, "and emphasized with the terrible power of divine pain."[107] However evangelical in tone and fervency the sermon may be, noticeably absent from it is any mention of Christ actually paying the penalty for sin in a substitutionary way. Brooks argues simply that God is just, but also forgives, and the death of Christ is the means of proclaiming that message. Any person, therefore, "may come to God with a perfect assurance that God will forgive him, and introduce him through the gate of forgiveness into a better and diviner life, and lead him on from holiness to holiness, and bring him at last to untold glory."[108]

In another soteriological sermon, called "The Conqueror from Edom," Brooks makes several statements that resonate with traditional evangelicalism, maintaining that "salvation must be His and His alone," and "Christianity is in its very nature exclusive."[109] He emphasizes the Devil as a personal enemy and the pervasiveness of sin as the "undying foe" that leaves humanity "helpless."[110] Brooks even affirms, "The whole work of the Saviour has relation to and issues from the fact of sin. If there had been no sin there would have been no Saviour."[111] He brings his message to a climax by proclaiming,

> Only this I know is the burden and soul of it all, this truth—that sin is a horrible, strong, positive thing, and that not even divinity grapples with him and subdues him except in strife and pain. . . . This symbol of the blood—and by and by, when we turn from the Old Testament to the New, from the prophecy to the fulfillment, we find that it was not only the enemy's blood, but His own blood too, that stained the victorious deliverer's robes—this symbol of the blood bears this great truth, which has been the power of salvation to millions of hearts, and which must make this conqueror the Saviour of your heart too, the truth that only in self-sacrifice and suffering could even God conquer sin.[112]

107. Ibid., 266.
108. Ibid., 267–68.
109. Brooks, "Conqueror from Edom," 41.
110. Ibid., 47–50.
111. Ibid., 50.
112. Ibid., 53.

Yet again, without any mention of a real atonement, substitution, or payment, Brooks claims, "Out of that love born of His suffering comes the new impulse after a holy life; and so when we stand at last purified by the power of grateful obedience, it shall be said of us, binding our holiness and escape from our sin close to our Lord's struggle with sin for us, that we have 'washed our robes and made them white in the blood of the Lamb.'"[113] Brooks stands at the very doorstep of the traditional evangelical doctrine of atonement, but does not enter it. He concludes the sermon with the following words:

> And so what is the fruit of the salvation that the divine Saviour brings to the souls of men? It does not finish them at once; it does not fill and stock their lives with heavenly richness in a moment. But it does just this. It sets them free; it takes off the load of sin; it gives us a new chance; it secures forgiveness, and says to the poor soul, that has been thinking there was no use of trying to stagger on with such a load, Go on; your burden is removed. Go on, go up to the home that you were made for, and the life in God.[114]

Brooks recognized "some sort of conflict and victory, wrought in sacrifice and pain"[115] in the death of Christ, but he notably avoided the term "vicarious"—the most significant term of his era used for referring to substitutionary atonement. In fact, when Brooks did employ the term, he sounded a great deal like Bushnell, who commented, "What we call this redemption of mankind must bring them to the common standard. Executed by vicarious sacrifice in himself, it must also be issued in vicarious sacrifice in them."[116] Harp captures Bushnell's concept, observing that "this vicariousness of Jesus is echoed and illustrated in the lives of men in whom God is working and who seek to show others how to be reconciled to God. Thus the cross is exemplary more than it is really propitiatory; it is a call to Christians to take up a life of altruistic service and suffering for others, rather than meeting the demands of God's justice."[117] Brooks indeed followed such a line of thought, purporting that Jesus' death was vicarious because it "made possible for us the

---

113. Ibid., 53–54.

114. Ibid., 55.

115. Minyard, "Theology of Phillips Brooks," 99.

116. Bushnell, quoted in Smith, *Horace Bushnell*, 283.

117. Harp, *Brahmin Prophet*, 177.

same consecration and fulfillment of it that he achieved."[118] In another sermon, Brooks explains,

> As Christ's temptation was vicarious, and when He conquered He conquered for others beside Himself, so it is with us. There are men and women all around us who have got to meet the same temptations that we are meeting. Will it help them or not to know that we have met them and conquered them? Will it help us or not to know that if we conquer the temptation we conquer not for ourselves only, but for them? . . . The vicariousness of all of life! There is not one of us who has not some one more or less remotely fastened to his acts, concerning whom he may say, as Christ said, "For their sakes I sanctify myself."[119]

Conversionism

In Bebbington's quadrilateral, conversionism is the "belief that lives need to be changed," and such change occurs as people become "justified by faith."[120] Harp points out, though, the suspicious vacancy of the doctrine of justification by grace through faith alone in Brooks's thought, saying, "What is almost entirely absent from Brooks's sermons is a treatment of exactly *how* a guilty sinner is reckoned righteous by a gracious God."[121] Even Minyard's extensive systemization of Brooks's theology contains very little on the topics of justification, regeneration, and conversion.[122] Similar to his personal experience, the whole matter of conversion in Brooks's work remains a vague process that relies heavily on Bushnell's concept of Christian nurture.

The cross itself, for Brooks, lingers as a mystery "where the deeper battle goes on out of our sight" and, consequently, salvation happens when "from this Saviour there goes forth a Spirit which finds out the hearts of men and touches them and melts in with them and makes Himself a part of them, and spreads through every vein of all their life these two truths of the Christ: that God loves man and that man is his

---

118. Brooks, quoted in Allen, *Life and Letters*, 2:477.

119. Brooks, "First Sunday in Lent," 140–41.

120. Bebbington, *Evangelicalism in Modern Britain*, 3, 6.

121. Harp, *Brahmin Prophet*, 177.

122. Minyard only tags short discussions of these matters onto the larger sections titled "Christ and the Atonement" and "The Doctrine of Man." Minyard, "Theology of Phillips Brooks," 100–102, 138–42.

true self when he is filially serving God.''[123] Elsewhere, Brooks speaks of salvation as a return to true, natural life, describing that it is "not rescue from suffering, not plucking out of fire . . . but health—the cool, calm vigor of normal human life; the making of the man to be himself . . . this is salvation!"[124] His ideas of regeneration and conversion follow suit. While he was in Germany, Brooks outlined his view of regeneration:

> It is the need that every man should thus fulfill his own true life which makes the obligation, and must ultimately make for every man the attractiveness, of *duty*.
>
> While this is the distinctive New Testament Idea of Duty, the other Ideas of Duty have their true place. Always "mere morality," as it used to be called, is included and involved, not set aside by the Gospel. Such motives as the fear of the consequences of sin, the honorable gratitude to God, the regard for the well-being of humanity, the instinctive sense of the beauty of conforming to the moral law, are freely used to surround and sustain the central motive which comes of the soul's revealed possibilities. Indeed some of these motives may be considered only as other forms of this motive.
>
> The entrance into this deeper consciousness and into the motive power which it exercises is Regeneration, the *new* Birth.[125]

Along these same moralistic, nurturing lines come Brooks's thoughts on conversion. According to him,

> What is it that comes in that day when a man begins the Christian life? Across a resolution which may be hard or easy for him, he sets forth into a new way of living. . . . He who has been living alone begins to live with God. He who has been living for himself begins to live for other men. New motives are open within him; new tasks are spread before him. Old things are passed away; all things are become new. . . . If you want to make a man a Christian, how shall you begin? . . . Will you emphasize the moment of change so strongly that it shall seem as if, before that, as he had cared nothing for the Saviour, the Saviour also had cared nothing for him? No; you will tell him, if you know your blessed work, of a power which has been in his life from the moment that his life began.[126]

123. Brooks, *Mystery of Iniquity,* 16; idem, "Sunday after Christmas," 101.

124. Brooks, "Light of the World," 9.

125. Brooks, quoted in Allen, *Life and Letters,* 2:479.

126. Brooks, "New Experiences," 300–301.

Similarly and succinctly, Brooks elsewhere claims, "To open the eyes and find a Christ beside us,—not to go long journeys to discover a Christ with whom before we have had nothing to do,—this is the Christian conversion."[127] As a result, in his view, conversion consists of a growing acknowledgment of a previously existing relationship with Christ and a subsequent return to one's true and moral self.

Contrast Brooks's view of conversion with the more traditional evangelical view of Vinton, his childhood pastor. Vinton agreed that, in some sense, conversion represents a return to God's original plan for mankind and a call to duty, but he included the terminology of sin, depravity, and surrender as well. He never hinted that conversion is the realization of a previously present life, but spoke of a

> transaction by which a disobedient servant is reclaimed to his rightful lord and master; a rebel lays down his arms, subdued to the constitutional authority; a sinner led to find a Saviour. . . . So much as the sweet harmony of the world has been broken by this jarring element of sin, the only discord in it, is not the sense of beauty awakened when that harmony restored and the sin destroyed? Every conversion to Jesus Christ, tends, so far as it goes, to restore the original pattern of the creation, when God's smile reflected beauty from its unsinning and unpunished life; when order reigned unmarred, and all created beings gravitated towards God. It is beautiful, then, to see a depraved and offending creature return where his duty calls, and forswear his insurrection, and take his holy stand in the ranks of Christ's people.[128]

Brooks's soft stance on conversion—and atonement—sprang directly from his elevated view of humanity that he gleaned from romantic thought. He certainly acknowledged the malignancy of sin, calling it "an invasion of man's nature, something foreign to him, that he should be base and mean and low and sordid and foul."[129] Following Coleridge, however, Brooks did not believe that the Fall changed the essential goodness of the human soul, and he held quite strongly to his conviction that "every man is the child of God."[130] In fact, Brooks maintained

127. Brooks, "Opening of the Eyes," 212.

128. Vinton, *Sermons*, 37.

129. Brooks, "Need of Enthusiasm," 298.

130. Ibid., 300. This theme frequently is repeated in Brooks's sermons and essays. Minyard, "Theology of Phillips Brooks," 132. Coleridge states that the doctrine of total depravity exaggerates "the diseased weakness into an absolute privation of all freedom."

such a close relationship between God and man that he frequently spoke of the "intrinsic" and "essential divinity of human life," mentioning that humanity "belongs to God, that it is the utterance of God's life."[131] In one of his clearly anthropological sermons, titled "The Giant with the Wounded Heel" (based on Gen 3:15), Brooks forged a Pelagian, middle pathway between the Calvinistic view of original sin and the blind optimism of some romantics like William Ellery Channing:

> One calls humanity a hopeless brute. Another man calls humanity a triumphant angel. God in these words of Genesis says, "Neither, but a wounded, bruised, strong creature, not running, leaping, and shouting, often crawling and creeping in pain, but yet brave, with an inextinguishable certainty of ultimate success, fighting a battle which is full of pain, but is not desperate, sure ultimately to set his heel upon the adversary's head."[132]

In an insightful and surprisingly critical essay, Edward Abbot lucidly reports the ramifications of Brooks's anthropology on his soteriology. He attests,

> Some of us may not think that he always shows the Cross or the Saviour who hangs upon it in as strong a light as he would have done had he held a different view of sin and guilt and of the condition of man by nature, and had depicted Redemption against that dark background of depravity and condemnation which seems to find its indictment in Scripture and its evidence in human life, and of which he makes so little.[133]

Activism

Bebbington defines activism as the "expression of the gospel in effort," and claims that it is a sustained "leading characteristic of Evangelicals."[134] In the nineteenth century, Moody set the evangelical standard for activism, particularly with his extensive preaching crusades. He was not "averse to institutional solutions," as his prominent role in the Young Men's Christian Association demonstrates, but he insisted that even cooperative efforts should keep the "conversion of individuals at the center

---

Coleridge, *Aids to Reflection*, 196.

131. Brooks, "Need of Enthusiasm," 299.

132. Brooks, "Giant with the Wounded Heel," 95.

133. Abbott, *Phillips Brooks: A Memory*, 45.

134. Bebbington, *Evangelicalism in Modern Britain*, 3, 10.

of their mission."[135] A traditional evangelical concept of individual conversion—based upon a traditional evangelical anthropology—indeed
was the very aim of all his activity. In a sermon delivered in Boston, he
openly spoke of humanity as a failure, stating,

> [I]f Nicodemus, that moralist in Jerusalem, needed to be born
> again, so does every man in Boston. This idea, that you who are
> born in Boston don't need to be born again of the Spirit, comes
> from the Devil; it don't [sic] come from the Bible. You can't find
> that anywhere in the Scriptures; the moralist of Boston needs to
> be converted as much as the drunkard. "Except ye be converted,
> ye shall not enter into the kingdom of God."[136]

Brooks adopted a similar "one soul at a time" approach. He was sometimes criticized in the years after the Civil War for his silence on issues like
economic inequality and the need for societal structural change. While
he did participate in some organized reform efforts, such as the Women's
Suffrage Festival and the New England Society for the Suppression of
Vice, his deep confidence in social progress, rooted in his belief in the
goodness of humanity, "helped dull his commitment to social change."[137]
"The final unit is the man," according to Brooks, which makes "idola-
try of organic methods."[138] Perhaps only Frederick Maurice's notion of
humanity as a whole in *The Kingdom of Christ* helped to soften his stiff,
individualistic position.

   Brooks and Moody may have shared a similar individualism in regard to the "expression of the gospel in effort," but their grounds could
not have been more different. Moody declared, "I look upon this world
as a wrecked vessel. God has given me a lifeboat and said to me, 'Moody,
save all you can.'" In great contrast, Brooks declared, "Stop doing your
sin, no matter how mechanical it seems, and then take up your duty,
whatever you can do to make the world more bright and good."[139] For
Moody, activism meant saving souls from sin. For Brooks, activism
meant urging souls to morality.

---

135. Harp, *Brahmin Prophet*, 137.
136. Moody, quoted in Daniels, *Moody*, 411–12.
137. Harp, *Brahmin Prophet*, 132–35.
138. Brooks, quoted in Harp, *Brahmin Prophet*, 134.
139. Brooks, "Duty of the Business Man," 87.

Evaluation

Minyard's estimate that Brooks did not innovate new doctrinal formulations, but rather "chose to universalize the traditional expressions with larger outlooks," only veils the true influences behind Brooks's thought.[140] The romantic overtones distinguishing Brooks from traditional nineteenth-century evangelicals in the aforementioned doctrinal categories present a mere microcosm of the extent to which the waves of romanticism flowed through him. Steve Wilkins and Alan Padgett wonder openly whether romanticism became the "tail that wags the dog," resulting in a religion that "can no longer be recognized as Christianity."[141] When set against Bebbington's quadrilateral, it becomes clear that Brooks used evangelical terminology, but filled the terms with meanings largely provided by romantic philosophy.

Surprisingly, though, many of Brooks's biographers caricature him as a dedicated evangelical. Allen concludes that when Brooks graduated from Virginia Theological Seminary, he "freely accepted the leading truths which are known as Evangelical."[142] Woolverton contends that Brooks remained "surprisingly loyal to the reformed theology," and E. Clowes Chorley holds that "Brooks never drifted from the heart of Evangelical religion."[143] Interestingly, Jerome F. Politzer purports that Brooks's sermons "carry on the great tradition of evangelical conviction," and then summarizes—under that category—a system of Brooks's thought that includes nothing of the Fall, original sin, or substitutionary atonement.[144] Such a label seems puzzling in light of the above comparison with Bebbington's quadrilateral, but some preliminary contributing factors can be identified.

First of all, Brooks's persistent theological ambiguity counts as one major factor. His ambiguity, when combined with his evangelical fervency and consistent use of evangelical terminology, causes some analysts to make unmerited assumptions about his beliefs. In a 1949 dissertation on Brooks, David White excerpts portions of Brooks's sermons that echo evangelical thought, inserts the necessary doctrinal propositions,

140. Minyard, "Theology of Phillips Brooks," 23.

141. Wilkins and Padgett, *Faith & Reason*, 39.

142. Allen, *Life and Letters*, 1:315–16.

143. Woolverton, *Education of Phillips Brooks*, 105; Chorley, *Men and Movements*, 299.

144. Politzer, "Theological Ideas," 157–69.

and affirms that these truths "became the underlying ideas in all that he said."[145] For instance, White claims that Brooks held to an evangelical view of conversion by citing the following from Brooks:

> [W]hen the possession of the soul by Christ is called the "New Birth," one of the meanings of that name is this, that then there is a reassertion of personality, and the soul which had lost itself in the slavery of the multitude finds itself again in the obedience of Christ.[146]

White determines from this quotation that "man's part in the atonement was to accept the sacrifice of Christ by repentance and faith" without noting the utter absence of any atonement concept in Brooks's sermon.[147]

Second, historiographical error—perhaps as an outgrowth of bias—constitutes another factor in the labeling of Brooks as an evangelical. Allen's assessment of Brooks as an evangelical places an inordinately high priority on the academic papers that Brooks wrote during his seminary training, apparently overlooking the fact that these essays were written for course credit at an evangelical institution. Treating them as definitive statements with respect to Brooks's theology, Allen notes that they render him to be

> a theologian, versed in the intricacies of theology as a system, knowing his way easily from one department to another. So well was he indoctrinated that he made no technical mistakes; never contradicted any formal teaching of creeds or articles of formularies; never erred through ignorance, or made a theological blunder; never asserted as a new truth what had been condemned by any reputable authority as untrue.[148]

Harp rightly insists, however, that Brooks's coursework must be weighed against his private notebooks and personal correspondence during these same years, which decidedly point away from traditional evangelical thought and more toward romanticism.[149] As another example, consider Wiersbe's assertion that, although Brooks avoided "typical evangelical . . . clichés" in the pulpit, he still taught "evangeli-

---

145. White, "Preaching of Phillips Brooks," 69.

146. Brooks, "Fire and the Calf," 62.

147. White, "Preaching of Phillips Brooks," 89.

148. Allen, *Life and Letters,* 1:313–15.

149. Harp, *Brahmin Prophet,* 37.

cal doctrine" in his Bible classes, despite clear historical evidence that Brooks actually scrutinized evangelicalism in his classes.[150] Without citing any support, Wiersbe continues, "We wish he had emphasized the cross and the resurrection more, because he certainly believed in them."[151]

Third, a matrix of issues surrounding Brooks's life and ministry has created an evangelical aura about him that proves difficult to remove. His avoidance of controversy, his public cooperation with evangelicals like Moody, and his broad appeal combine to create a lingering evangelical reverence for him, which tends to soften any charges of doctrinal inconsistency.[152] Other factors—such as his mother's firm Calvinism, his education at an evangelical seminary, and Vinton's influence during his childhood—may play into these evangelical estimations of Brooks, too.

The most significant factor, though, in labeling Brooks as an evangelical results from the theologically ambivalent way that the term "evangelical" came to be employed in the late nineteenth century. By 1887, for instance, the Evangelical Alliance included a theological range broad enough that numerous otherwise incompatible theologies mingled together to carry out a distinctively social agenda.[153] Viewed through the lens of Bebbington's quadrilateral, it seems that "activism" trumped the other three components in defining who were and who were not evangelical. Yet, with the discrepancies between Brooks and the doctrines of historic evangelicalism, Harp rightly and assertively requests a revision of this "received view" of Brooks.[154] In light of the foregoing, Brooks indeed may be quite confidently termed as a romantic Christian, and perhaps even as a Christianized romantic.

ROMANTICISM IN THE HOMILETIC OF PHILLIPS BROOKS

While the next chapter presents a more thorough theological inquiry into Brooks's definition of preaching as "truth through personality," a discussion of romanticism's overall influence on him remains incomplete

150. Wiersbe, "Preacher of Truth and Life," 16. Allen reveals, though, that Brooks actually denied the "unerring accuracy" of the Bible in his adult class. Allen, *Life and Letters*, 3:95.

151. Wiersbe, "Preacher of Truth and Life," 16.

152. Harp, *Brahmin Prophet*, 91–93.

153. Wacker, "Holy Spirit and the Spirit of the Age," 268.

154. Harp, "Young Phillips Brooks," 652; idem, *Brahmin Prophet*, 38.

without mentioning—in a preliminary way—some of its more evident effects on his preaching. Preaching, especially Protestant preaching, was "the most influential form of rhetoric in nineteenth century America."[155] Harp cites several significant factors that contribute to preaching's prominence in the period, including its centrality in Protestantism, the popularity of itinerant evangelists, and the oratorical political atmosphere of antebellum America.[156] Typical evangelical preaching followed along the old Puritan lines of exposition and application, maintaining the goal of preaching the Bible and its doctrine in a clear, organized, and systematic way. "The sermon almost invariably had two main divisions," remarks Brastow, "with numerous subdivisions, the first, theoretic, containing the discussion, which was generally argumentative, the second, practical, called 'improvement' or 'use.' Its anchorage ground was the theology of the church or of some school, and even the Biblical material . . . became a vehicle for conveying this theology."[157]

John Albert Broadus stood as an evangelical exemplar among late-nineteenth-century preachers. His personal study of a particular scriptural passage was thorough; his sermon structure was simple and clear; and his delivery was natural and nearly extemporaneous.[158] For example, in a sermon based on Matthew 1:21, his outline follows the text directly: (1) He shall save; (2) He shall save His people; and (3) From their sins. Exegetical, doctrinal, and applicable material appears under each heading.[159] Broadus set forth his vision for preaching in his magnum opus, *A Treatise on the Preparation and Delivery of Sermons*:

> To interpret and apply his text in accordance with its real meaning, is one of the preacher's most sacred duties. He stands before the people for the very purpose of teaching and exhorting them out of the Word of God. He announces a particular passage of God's Word as his text with the distinctly implied understanding that from this his sermon will be drawn—if not always its various thoughts, yet certainly its general subject.[160]

155. Howden, "Pulpit Leads the World," 169.

156. Harp, *Brahmin Prophet*, 109.

157. Brastow, *Modern Pulpit*, 125.

158. Turnbull, *From the Close of the Nineteenth Century*, 106–7.

159. Ibid., 108–9.

160. Broadus, *Treatise*, 32.

In Episcopal circles, McIlvaine and Tyng utilized a method similar to that of Broadus, and brought great emphasis to Christ's substitutionary atonement as the central message of preaching. In his booklet, *The Work of Preaching Christ*, McIlvaine states that neglecting the cross of Christ in preaching is worse "than even the introduction of some positive error" and brings an "awful condemnation" to the preacher who is "essentially defective at the very heart of the great work committed to us!"[161]

The influence of romanticism—coupled with American individualism—drew many preachers away from the doctrinal format, however, and toward a more experiential and practical approach. As romanticism rendered a form of Christianity centered upon subjective feelings and moral achievement, the traditional evangelical scheme became "inappropriate" as the "quickening of the religious sentiment was widely held to be a better aim for the preacher than the inculcation of a fixed body of doctrine."[162] Literary, emotive, and imaginative preachers quickly emerged, and Brooks became a pioneer among them. Brooks's homiletic, observes Harp, "served to disconnect the experimental from the dogmatic by denigrating the latter and injecting a new vigor into the former."[163]

Brooks's experiential approach to homiletics broke away decisively from traditional evangelical methodologies. In his *Lectures on Preaching*, he nearly ignores matters pertaining to sermon composition and structure, teaching only that "every sermon must have a solid rest on Scripture, and the pointedness which comes of a clear subject, and the conviction which belongs to well-thought argument, and the warmth that proceeds from earnest appeal."[164] While working under the guise of evangelical terminology, though, Brooks steers the focus almost entirely toward the human element in preaching. For instance, Brooks suggests that a sermon should "fasten itself to the authority of Scripture," yet encourages preachers to pick a topic before choosing a text, and purports that the selection depends "upon the richness of a man's own life."[165] He additionally requires preaching doctrine, but defines it simply as "making Christ plain."[166]

---

161. McIlvaine, *Work of Preaching Christ*, 11–12.

162. Buell, "Unitarian Movement," 180, 167.

163. Harp, *Brahmin Prophet*, 115.

164. Brooks, *Lectures on Preaching*, 131.

165. Ibid., 130, 149.

166. Ibid., 128.

In Brooks's model, the preacher's personality, the preacher's personal development, and the relationship between the preacher and the congregation become the chief concerns and central dynamics of preaching.[167] He calls a sermon "man and paper together," and says that the key to style is the "cultivation of the man . . . to a more generous and exalted life."[168] Brooks claims, "More than its most ingenious invention or its most highly organized government, a man's best sermon is the best utterance of his life."[169] In this way, his romanticized "truth through personality" model switches "the primary focus from an external message toward the subjective character of the messenger appealing to the religious sentiment of his auditors."[170]

Along with a substantial revision of sermon methodology, romanticism caused Brooks to rethink the content and purpose of preaching. In his lectures, Brooks sustains the same ambivalence pertaining to salvation and atonement found in his sermons. While using familiar evangelical terminology, he again gently shifts the locus of authority away from external doctrinal content toward the individual conscience:

> But when you feel the anxious wish of men and women really seeking after truth, when the cry "What must I do to be saved?" sounds in your quickened ears from all the intent and silent pews, then is the time when you really learn how wide and various salvation is. The revival and the inquiry room must always widen a man's conception of Christianity, and they are only the emphatic expressions of what is always present and may always be felt in every congregation. . . . The more you think of your congregation as seekers after salvation, to whom you are to open the sacred doors, the more ready you will be to see each entering into a salvation peculiarly his own.[171]

Elsewhere, Brooks freely asserts that the purpose of preaching is "for men's salvation," but immediately adds that "the idea of salvation has never been entirely uniform or certain."[172] Without uniformity or certainty of salvific doctrine, the truth to be delivered through personality

---

167. Ibid., 73–74, 208, 277–78.

168. Ibid., 148.

169. Ibid., 135.

170. Harp, *Brahmin Prophet*, 117.

171. Brooks, *Lectures*, 204–5.

172. Ibid., 32.

becomes starkly anthropocentric—the "human side of every truth."[173] He describes the value of the human soul as the very power and central motive for preaching, and even observes that human interaction offers a source for preaching.[174] With a "childlike hope in human nature," preaching in Brooks's vein reduces faith to "personal loyalty" and aims toward "personal perfectness" by proclaiming "character, which we know is the one thing in man which God values and for which Christ labored and lived and died."[175] Instead of preaching to save man from his sinful nature by Christ's blood, Brooks's model attempts to awaken in man the "stronger nature" by shaping character.[176] Romanticism, therefore, which is so present in Brooks's theology, flows freely through his homiletical theory.

CONCLUSION

The life, ministry, and preaching of Phillips Brooks closely mirror the rise of romanticism in nineteenth-century American Christianity. The seedlings of historic evangelical doctrine—planted in him by his mother, by Vinton, and by Virginia Theological Seminary—withered quickly under the "new light" offered by the romantic influences of Coleridge, Bushnell, Maurice, and others.[177] These influences brought ramifications for his theology that, in turn, greatly affected his homiletical theory. Like his theology, his homiletical theory represents a deep, fundamental divergence from historic evangelicalism. The intense presence of romanticism within Brooks's definition of preaching as "truth through personality" indeed offers a fundamental revision of Protestant homiletics—one that necessitates a deeper, theological analysis.

173. Ibid., 46.

174. Ibid., 255–56, 47.

175. Ibid., 127–28, 261, 263.

176. Ibid., 79, 204.

177. In one sermon, Brooks refers to historic doctrines as old and partial truths from which "new truth" and "new light" must progress. Brooks, *Year Book*, 204.

3

Incarnation and Preaching

Having jettisoned the major tenets of traditional evangelical-ism, Phillips Brooks nonetheless construed his romantic convictions in a Christian way by latching on to one key Christian doctrine: the incarnation of Jesus Christ. The doctrine became his "leading motive, and the ground principle of his theology and of his life."[1] It was for him the "final, non-negotiable, bedrock doctrine" that formed both the "hub" and "silent presupposition" of all his preaching.[2] "Oh to preach a great sermon on the Incarnation!" he aspired in one of his notebooks.[3] Beyond the centrality of the incarnation in Brooks's theology, though, the doctrine held pivotal sway in his homiletical theory. In fact, he called preaching "the continuation, out to the minutest ramifications . . . of that personal method which the Incarnation itself had involved."[4] His entire approach to ministry rested on the principle that "there is no real leadership of people for a preacher or a pastor except that which comes as the leadership of the Incarnation came."[5] Brooks's very definition of preaching as "truth through personality" constitutes a restatement of his incarnation formula in homiletical terms. This chapter thus identifies how he formulated the incarnation; traces its centrality in his theology; and demonstrates the way in which his formulation and application of the incarnation dominate his definition of preaching.

---

1. Brooks, quoted in Allen, *Life and Letters*, 3:101. Brooks's biographers and analysts consistently note the primacy of the incarnation for Brooks. Minyard, "Theology of Phillips Brooks," 62.

2. Harp, *Brahmin Prophet*, 211; Ensley, "Phillips Brooks and the Incarnation," 351.

3. Brooks, quoted in Allen, *Life and Letters*, 3:103.

4. Brooks, *Lectures*, 7.

5. Ibid., 85.

PHILLIPS BROOKS'S INCARNATION FORMULA

Properly speaking, the incarnation is "the act whereby the eternal Son of God, the Second Person of the Holy Trinity, without ceasing to be what he is, God the Son, took into union with himself what he before that act did not possess, a human nature," such that "Jesus Christ was *one* person with a divine nature and a human nature."[6] Phillips Brooks formulated the incarnation in a generally orthodox way, albeit nondogmatic and loosely defined. In typical fashion, his approach "could be expected to satisfy the average conservative layman" while, at the same time, allowing "a broad and liberal interpretation."[7] He affirmed the bare essentials of an orthodox construction—namely, the divinity and humanity of Jesus Christ. "It was a true Incarnation," Brooks believed. "It was a real bringing of God in the flesh."[8] He plainly avoided the errors of Arianism, docetism, and adoptionism, but he also openly shunned any technical discussion of the way that the divine and human natures fit together in Christ:

> But what the internal preparation for the Incarnation was, by the very nature of the case we cannot know. "A body has Thou prepared Me"! How that body was prepared and the God-man made possible; how the new nature was made ready and the Word made flesh; how God approached that marvelous period in His eternity when He put on the guise of a creature and came as Christ—all this who dares to tell, who even dares to conjecture! To know that, one must uncover all the mysteries of the divine and human natures, one must know all the most secret and sacred processes of heaven and earth; nay, one must *be* God—no less than that.[9]

The incarnation remained a mystery for Brooks, and he was not willing to engage in the details laid out at Nicea and Chalcedon.[10] Without employing the careful distinctions made by the historic creeds, however, Brooks sometimes envisioned an incarnation concept that bordered on monophysite Eutychianism—the error that Christ's divine and human

---

6. Reymond, "Incarnation," 555–56. See also Hodge, *Anthropology*, 378–94.

7. Minyard, "Theology of Phillips Brooks," 90.

8. Brooks, *Year Book*, 361.

9. Brooks, "Fourth Sunday in Advent," 63–64. Interestingly, those who were opposed to Brooks's nomination as bishop charged him with Arianism. Allen, *Life and Letters*, 3:425.

10. Minyard, "Theology of Phillips Brooks," 87–89.

natures combined to create a third kind of nature.[11] In a sermon titled "The Eternal Humanity," Brooks observes,

> Christ is the Divinely human, the humanly Divine. It is the Deity endowed with a peculiar human sympathy, showing by a genuine brotherhood the experience of man. That is to say, there are two words: God and Man. One describes pure deity, the other pure humanity. Christ is a word not identical with either, but including both. It is the Deity in which the Humanity has part; it is Humanity in which the Deity resides. It is that special mediatorial nature which has its own double wearing of both, the ability to stand between and reconcile the separated manhood and divinity.[12]

He states elsewhere,

> There is one whole, homogenous Being which is our Christ. The human never acts without the divine, the divine never without the human. There is not divine and human, as we sometimes say, that splits and mars His perfect nature. Not a God and a man, that is two—but a God-man, one supreme and perfect and constant nature, . . . a divine humanity, and humanized Divinity.[13]

On the whole, Alfred Minyard estimates that Brooks moved with "apparent freedom" with regard to the incarnation, "expressing himself in terms often suggestive of less orthodox Christologies."[14] He indeed "held to the form of creedal orthodoxy while giving it liberal interpretation in terms sufficiently ambiguous as to defy exact categorization."[15]

Other components of Brooks's incarnation formula, while clinging to orthodox essentials, contain striking modifications. First of all, Brooks affirmed that the incarnation was a miraculous event that occurred in real history, but he simultaneously believed in its "naturalness":

> The wonderful thing about this sense of Divinity as it appears in Jesus is its naturalness, the absence of surprise or of any feeling of violence. . . . [T]his new life, into which God comes, seems to

11. For helpful discussions regarding Eutychianism and its refutation by the early creeds, see MacLeod, *Person of Christ*, 183–85; Akin, *Theology for the Church*, 521–30; Grudem, *Systematic Theology*, 554–64.

12. Brooks, "Eternal Humanity," 311.

13. Brooks, quoted in Minyard, "Theology of Phillips Brooks," 90.

14. Minyard, "Theology of Phillips Brooks," 91.

15. Ibid.

be the most quietly, naturally human life that was ever seen upon the earth. It glides into its place like sunlight. It seems to make it evident that God and man are essentially so near together, that the meeting of their natures in the life of a God-man is not strange.[16]

In this way, the incarnation depicts "miraculousness" and "quietness." According to Brooks, "The breakage through the ordinary laws of nature's life seems natural and fitting."[17] The third stanza of his famous Christmas carol, "O Little Town of Bethlehem," portrays this theme:

> *How silently, how silently*
> *The wondrous gift is given!*
> *So God imparts to human hearts*
> *The blessings of his heaven.*
> *No ear may hear his coming,*
> *But in this world of sin,*
> *Where meek souls will receive him,*
> *Still the dear Christ enters in.*

Second, Brooks plainly affirmed the preexistence of Christ, but added the notion of Jesus' preexistent humanity. For him, Christ did not become human when he was born on earth, but rather continued to be what he is forever. In "The Eternal Humanity," Brooks purports,

> Now, if we can comprehend that truth at all, it must be evident that before man was made the man-type existed in God. In some part of His perfect nature there was the image of what the new creation was to be. Already, before man trod the garden in the high glory of his new Godlikeness, the pattern of the thing he was to be existed in the nature of Him who was to make him. Before the clay was fashioned and the breath was given, this humanity existed in the Divinity; already there was a union of the Divine and human; and thus already there was an eternal Christ. . . . What if there be a Christ . . . who only brought out into exhibition when He came in human flesh that genuine human brotherhood which had been in him forever? . . . Yes, "from the beginning" there had been a second person in the Trinity,—a Christ, whose nature included the man-type.[18]

16. Brooks, quoted in Allen, *Life and Letters*, 3:105.

17. Ibid., 3:111.

18. Brooks, "Eternal Humanity," 312–14.

Brooks never pursued the logical problems presented by these modifications—such as the place of an uncreated, preexistent humanity in the nature of the Trinity—but these alterations were more than the fruit of a fanciful mind. One may detect undertones of Hegelian synthesis and perhaps even a faint echo of Strauss's mythological take on the incarnation, but Brooks never "made any effort to understand the purpose of Hegel," and "rejected the conception of Christ offered by Strauss."[19] Brooks did, however, welcome John Robert Seeley's book, *Ecce Homo*—a seminal work in the Broad Church movement. Seeley brushed aside critical inquiry into the Bible and miracles to highlight Christ as the great figure and perfect example, whom humans should imitate, thereby raising "enthusiasm" for humanity.[20] Seeley's work confirmed Brooks's core conviction that "man is a child of God," and evidently had a significant influence on Brooks's thoughts about the incarnation.[21] Consequently, Brooks's modifications to Christ's incarnation appear to reflect and support his major anthropological precommitments.

THE CENTRALITY OF THE INCARNATION
IN PHILLIPS BROOKS'S THEOLOGY

Just as the lyrics of Brooks's well-known Christmas carol offer a glimpse into his incarnation formula, so his formula itself opens the window into the whole of his theology—his theological methodology, stance, and structure. On the one hand, Brooks's incarnation formula reveals his propensity to construe all doctrine in an anthropocentric way. On the other hand, Brooks's dogged insistence on the historical and miraculous fact of the incarnation prevents his Christology (and anthropology) from descending completely into Hegelian synthetic monism or other forms of transcendentalism. Brooks indeed extended the incarnation to all humanity, but nonetheless maintained Christ's uniqueness as the only perfect incarnation. In an essay dealing with the new theism, Brooks claims, "For the New Testament is always just on the brink of pantheism, and is only saved from it by the intense personality of Jesus."[22] On balance, Brooks's incarnation formula keeps him within the realm of

19. Allen, *Life and Letters,* 2:471, 338.

20. Seeley, *Ecce Homo,* 435–46.

21. Brooks, "Need of Enthusiasm," 297–99. See also Allen, *Life and Letters,* 2:339–40.

22. Brooks, "New Theism," 158.

Christianity, but simultaneously serves as a primary tool for advancing his exalted, romantic anthropology. In Brooks's scheme, Christ's incarnation—applied anthropocentrically—forms the central axis around which all his theology revolves. "However much he may have been guided unconsciously by his regard of man," Minyard writes with respect to Brooks, "his avowed basis of approach to divine truth was through the Incarnation. Out of the Incarnation came his distinctive thought of God and man and Christ."[23]

Most Christian theological systems begin with the doctrine of revelation and proceed in the order of the doctrine of God, anthropology, and soteriology. Brooks's system, however—rooted in romanticism and structured around the incarnation—forces a different order of analysis. Anthropology assumes second place only behind the incarnation, and following these doctrines come the categories of revelation and truth, the doctrine of God, and soteriology. Viewing the incarnational nuances in each of these doctrinal areas unveils the fundamental theological ideas present within his definition of preaching as "truth through personality."

The Incarnation as the Model for Anthropology

As much as the incarnation exists as a doctrine about Christ, in Brooks's thought it remains equally and essentially a doctrine about humanity. Brooks so intimately connected his doctrine of Christ with his anthropology that "he came to his concept of Christ by way of his admiration of humanity," and his "concept of Christ enabled him to see man in a new divine dimension."[24] In Brooks's *Lectures on Preaching*, he contends that the "Incarnation reveals the essential dignity of that nature into union with which the Deity could so marvelously enter," and this it does by showing that "God and man are essentially so near together."[25]

In a sermon titled "The Candle of the Lord" (based on Prov 20:27), Brooks opens with a vivid illustration of a candle that is "glorified by the fire and the fire is manifested by the candle." He later explains that "God is the fire of this world," and "the spirit of man is the candle." Hence, the nature of humanity "corresponds to the nature of God." Otherwise, the

---

23. Minyard, "Theology of Phillips Brooks," 63.

24. Ibid., 130.

25. Brooks, *Lectures*, 278; idem, quoted in Allen, *Life and Letters*, 3:105.

fire could not light the candle.[26] By mentioning correspondence, though, Brooks has significantly more in mind than humanity's bearing of God's image. According to him, the historical and miraculous fact that "God *did* become man" plainly shows that "manhood must be essentially capacious of divinity" and, in some sense, in unity with divinity.[27] Brooks asserts in an Advent sermon, "Christ came not merely to man, but *into* man; and that was possible because the manhood into which He entered was 'His own,' had original and fundamental unity with His Godhood, was made in the image of God."[28] Brooks indeed held humanity and divinity so closely that the incarnation became "God's commentary on that verse in Genesis, 'In the image of God created He man.'"[29] In an address presented at the 1888 Evangelical Alliance meeting, Brooks described "the essential divinity of human life, that it belongs to God, that it is the utterance of God's life."[30]

By casting Christ's incarnation in a distinctly anthropological way, Brooks elevated humanity to the romantic ideal that he gleaned from Seeley and Frederick Maurice. Francis Ensley maintains that Brooks universalized the doctrine and made it "a law of the universe of which the Life in Galilee is the one supreme illustration."[31] Brooks indeed thought that the "sum work of the Incarnation" shows that "man, and every man, is the child of God."[32] This theme is repeated throughout Brooks's preaching:

> He calls Himself the Son of God and He calls us God's sons. There is no confusion. His Sonship stands above our sonship always. Not one of us may say, as He says, "He that hath seen Me hath seen the Father." And yet all of us, because we are able to see the Father in Him, know ourselves truly sharers of His sonship.[33]

> When we say that every man has in him a true spiritual element, what we really mean is that every man is a child of God.[34]

26. Brooks, "Candle of the Lord," 1–4.

27. Brooks, "Second Sunday in Advent," 27.

28. Ibid., 26.

29. Brooks, "Eternal Humanity," 314; idem, "Second Sunday in Advent," 27.

30. Brooks, "Need of Enthusiasm," 299.

31. Ensley, "Phillips Brooks and the Incarnation," 356–57.

32. Brooks, *Influence of Jesus*, 12.

33. Brooks, "Trinity Sunday," 331–32.

34. Brooks, "Spiritual Man," 300.

When asked if Jesus' sonship differed from that of humanity in terms of kind or degree, he replied, "Surely one of degree, and that when great enough virtually becomes one in kind. He is the only perfect Son of the Father."[35] As a result, the potential to live a divine life and achieve greater sonship exists in all humanity. Brooks felt that the person "who sees God in Christ sees also himself and learns his own capacities as he receives the God whom Christ makes known to him."[36]

The Incarnation as the Source of Revelation and Truth

Brooks readily affirmed the core, inseparable Christian beliefs that "God is and God speaks."[37] The Lord is a revealing God, and there has never been "a time in all the past eternity when that which supremely Is has not spoken and sent Himself abroad."[38] At the beginning of a Wednesday-evening lecture delivered in 1880, though, Brooks preempted his discussion of the Scriptures by declaring that God's revelation occurs primarily "to a *Person*, because it is of a *Person*. Nothing but personality can really alter a personality."[39] The personality through which God reveals himself, then, is Jesus Christ. "Christ is the true Revelation of God," according to Brooks, "and the Bible gets its value from being the description of Christ."[40] Brooks felt that religion itself is not "a scheme of truth to be believed," but "a person to be believed in."[41] In fact, Brooks went as far as professing that religious belief, based on external forms of authority, actually "loses the clear conviction of the present Christ."[42] In Brooks's thought, therefore, Christ's incarnation forms the basis for all concepts of revelation.

Because Brooks's incarnation formula necessarily implies the "vast capacity of man," however, humans become a means of revelation as well.

---

35. Brooks, quoted in Minyard, "Theology of Phillips Brooks," 81. Another account of the same event slightly changes the question concerning whether the divinity (not merely sonship) of Jesus differs from that of humanity in terms of kind or degree, and records Brooks replying only, "In degree." Abbott, "The Supernatural," 583.

36. Brooks, "Second Sunday in Advent," 331.

37. Brooks, "Living Epistles," 111; idem, "Literature and Life," 461.

38. Brooks, "Living Epistles," 111.

39. Brooks, quoted in Allen, *Life and Letters*, 3:94–95.

40. Ibid., 3:95.

41. Brooks, "Pulpit and Popular Skepticism," 74.

42. Brooks, "Orthodoxy," 188.

The "great truth of the Incarnation" is "that a perfectly pure obedient humanity might utter divinity, might be the transparent medium through which even God might show Himself."[43] First of all, humanity reveals God simply by existing as children of God. According to a journal that Brooks wrote during a trip to Germany,

> God's first revelation of Himself must be in human nature itself. . . . There is here the first appearance of the truth that man is the *Child of God*. Both the wish and the possibility of God to show Himself to man in man's own nature are involved in the Idea of Childship. . . .
>   [In] man's finding God's first witness in himself (i.e., in man), there is always a half-consciousness that it must be *in human life* that the truest and fullest and deepest revelation of God is given.[44]

Second, humanity reveals God by bearing the image of God. In Brooks's essay, "The New Theism," he remarks that a deeper study of manhood aids in conceiving God:

> Not this man or that man with his partialness and fixed simplicity, but the universal manhood with its multitudinousness . . . that is the man which was made in God's image and by whose study the image of God may dimly open again upon the soul. We create first an artificial simplicity for our individual life, and we assert that only in such an individuality as that is there a real personality. The first enlargement of such a narrow conception as that is in the necessity of conceiving of the personality of man. The next is in the even deeper necessity of conceiving of the personality of God.[45]

Due to the fact that humans exist as God's children and bear his image, they acquire knowledge of God through instinct and introspection. "Man does not seem to reach the idea of God by a conscious process," but the notion of God instead "seems self-born, a direct impulse of the heart of man."[46] Following Samuel Taylor Coleridge and Frederick Maurice, Brooks believed that the spirit of faith resides very deeply in human nature—so deeply that intellectual skepticism cannot eradicate

---

43. Brooks, quoted in Allen, *Life and Letters*, 2:372.
44. Ibid., 2:474.
45. Brooks, "New Theism," 159–60.
46. Brooks, quoted in Allen, *Life and Letters,* 2:472.

it.[47] Developing this natural instinct of God into an actual consciousness of God occurs, though, by tracing the presence of "will" from the self to God:

> [T]he human mind cannot conceive of any original force except *will*. We learn it from observation of our human wills. Every other force is secondary. It is moved by something else behind it. But will is absolute and original. It admits no explanation. It is final in itself. And so when this marvelous problem of the universe confronts us, there is one and only one word which can suggest for it an adequate beginning or a competent government and that is *will*. Somewhere, sometime *will* must have touched these wheels, because in *will* alone in all the universe is there any creative power.[48]

Futhermore,

> Man finds only one stopping place in tracing back the claim of cause and effect in his own activity. That stopping place is in what seems to him to be truly an uncaused cause. When, then, he pictures to himself the stopping place of the chain of cause and effect in the greater world of active life, then, too, he thinks that at the beginning must lie *will*.[49]

For this reason, Brooks approached the doctrine of revelation with a distinctly anthropocentric bent that is consistent with his incarnation formula.

His incarnational and anthropocentric concept of revelation involved significant implications for his views of authority, orthodoxy, and heresy. Brooks expressed acute discomfort with any appeal to external authoritative forms, arguing that "authority as the regal principle in Christian thought is very dangerous" and is "meaningless unless it involves a practical infallibility."[50] He considered authority to be a bad substitute for personal judgment, and always gave the individual conscience supremacy in all matters of truth. In a keenly written essay, "Authority and Conscience," Brooks initially places authority and conscience in opposition to each other, and then declares conscience to be the victor. He comments:

47. Brooks, "Pulpit and Popular Skepticism," 69; Harp, *Brahmin Prophet*, 172.
48. Brooks, quoted in Minyard, "Theology of Phillips Brooks," 106.
49. Brooks, quoted in Allen, *Life and Letters*, 2:472.
50. Brooks, "Authority and Conscience," 116, 109.

> The principle of authority not merely emphasizes their fixity, but insists also that the mind of man must stand in an ever-fixed relation to them. The principle of conscience, accepting their fixity, recognizes and values the element of ever-advancing humanity, and in its ripening power expects, not new truth, but new knowledge of truth, to be emerging from the sea of ignorance forever. . . .
>
> The principle of authority looks back; the principle of conscience looks forward. . . . [T]he enthronement of authority . . . tends to kill enterprise; to cultivate sophistry; to perpetuate error; to magnify machineries and little things; and to hinder the progress of mankind.[51]

The "conscience," therefore, "not the authority, must be the final appeal; in the conscience, not in authority, must be the final warrant of all Christian truth."[52]

Making the individual conscience the final arbiter of truth required Brooks to revise conventional concepts of orthodoxy and heresy. In his thought, traditional orthodoxy represents nothing more than truth accepted by some means of external authority. Because external authority opposes personal conscience, he vigorously attacked the whole notion of orthodoxy. Brooks denigrated orthodoxy as the "premature conceit of certainty" and ultimately termed it an impersonal "false crystallization."[53] His essay on the matter contains a scathing condemnation:

> Against these meager uses [of orthodoxy] are to be set the vastly predominant evil which the whole principle of orthodoxy brings to personal freedom and reality, on one side, and to the purity and extension of truth upon the other. The indictment which can be sustained against it is tremendous. Orthodoxy begins by setting a false standard of life. It makes men aspire after soundness in faith rather than after richness in the truth. It exalts possessions over character, makes more of truths than of truthfulness, talks about truths as if they were things which were quite separated from the truth-holder, things which he might take in his hand and pass to his neighbor without their passing into and through his nature. It makes possible an easy transmission of truth, but only by the deadening of truth, as a butcher freezes meat in order to carry it across the sea. Orthodoxy discredits and discourages

51. Ibid., 116–17.
52. Ibid., 117.
53. Brooks, "Orthodoxy," 184–85, 193–94.

inquiry, and has made the name of "free-thinker," which ought to be a crown and glory, a stigma and disgrace. It puts men in the base and demoralizing position in which they apologize for seeking new truth. It is responsible for a large part of the defiant liberalism which not merely disbelieves the orthodox dogma, but disbelieves it with a sense of attempted wrong and of triumphant escape. It is orthodoxy, and not truth, which has done the persecuting. The inquisitions and dungeons and social ostracisms for opinion's sake belong to it. And in the truths which it holds it loses discrimination and a delicate sense of values, holding them not for their truth so much as for their use of their safety; it gives them a rude and general identity, and misses the subtle difference which makes each truth separate from every other. Orthodoxy deals in coarse averages. It makes of the world of truth a sort of dollar-store, wherein a few things are rated below their real value for the sake of making a host of others pass for more than they are worth, and in the lives of those who live by it orthodoxy makes no appeal to poetry or imagination. . . .

These are the evil things which the spirit of orthodoxy does and is, all of which sum themselves up in this—that it is born of fear, and has no natural heritage either from hope or love.[54]

Brooks obviously detached orthodoxy from truth. In fact, he considered orthodoxy and truth to be two concentric circles, with orthodoxy residing as a smaller circle inside the larger circle of truth. He believed that traditional orthodoxy often mistook itself for full truth, and contended that there should be "no lines of orthodoxy inside the lines of truth."[55]

In addition to Brooks's broadening of orthodoxy, he reconstructed the notion of heresy along distinctly moral lines. Because doctrines must be established on the grounds of moral consequence and not according to "abstract truth or falsehood, or their proof or disproof from the Bible," heresy comes about primarily through moral delinquency.[56] For him, heresy "is a subjective thing, an action of the will . . . its moral character is stamped upon it."[57] As an error of the will, heresy opposes faith and not necessarily a set of doctrines. In an essay supporting his

54. Ibid., 194–95.

55. Ibid., 185; idem, "Pulpit and Popular Skepticism," 67. For a contemporary endorsement of Brooks's view of orthodoxy, see Britton, "Breadth of Orthodoxy," 144–62.

56. Brooks, "Pulpit and Popular Skepticism," 73; idem, "Heresy," 8.

57. Brooks, "Heresy," 8.

idea of heresy, Brooks appeals to the assertion by Puritan John Milton that even truth can become heresy if wrongly held.

> He has brought the moral character of heresy to its complet-est statement. "Truth is compared in Scripture," he says, "to a streaming fountain; if her waters flow not in a perpetual progres-sion, they sink into a muddy pool of conformity and tradition. A man may be a heretic in the truth, and if he believes things only because his pastor says so, or the assembly so determines, without knowing other reason, though his belief may be true, yet the very truth he holds becomes his heresy."[58]

Consequently, Brooks felt that the dogmatic notion of heresy fails. "But," he claims, "if we can believe in the conscience, and God's willingness to enlighten it, and man's duty to obey its judgments, the moral conception of heresy sets definitely before us a goodness after which we may aspire, and a sin which we may struggle against and avoid."[59]

Revelation and truth, for Brooks, are ultimately and finally person-al. The greatest revelation of truth occurs in a Person, it comes to people, it resides in people, and is expressed by people. Hence, doctrine must primarily concern life and not abstractions. In his scheme, a doctrine is nothing but "a truth packed for transportation"[60] into life because truth must be

> transferred through character into life. . . . This is the great ideal. For where is force except in persons? What is the force of truth except as true men make it effective on their fellows? Where is the power of abstract ideas which, grasped into a mighty person-ality and grouped as the attributes of a personal God, make the universe tremble with terror or bow with a sob of love? "What is true?" said the weary Roman, too listless to care to judge between the true and the false in his despair of the abstract truth. "I am the Truth," answered the personal Saviour, and through His per-sonality the truth has saved the world.[61]

Moreover,

> I maintain that all impersonal truth, when it is acquired, however much it may do for the sharpening and stocking the brains and

58. Ibid., 15.
59. Ibid., 19.
60. Brooks, "Authority and Conscience," 114.
61. Brooks, "Purposes of Scholarship," 265.

improving the outward conditions of mankind, is as bad as use-
less as far as any immediate effect upon the character and tem-
perament is concerned. All truth must be brought, in order to be
effective, through a personal medium. . . .

All men are influenced mostly by *embodied truth*, by truth
coming to them through some relation of a fellow man.[62]

Brooks thought that "Christianity is to multitudes of people a purely abstract system," so he sought to reassert "its personal aspect." According
to him, the very essence of Christianity "is all built upon a person."[63]

The Incarnation as the Informant for the Doctrine of God

In the face of New England Unitarianism, Brooks remained firmly and
joyfully Trinitarian, even maintaining his position as something of a
protest against the "hard" and "tight" Unitarian perception of God.[64] For
Brooks, the Trinity "is an attempt to give richness, variety, mystery, internal relation, abundance, and freedom to the ideas of God."[65] He provided no technical or extended discussion of the nature of the Trinity,
and insisted that human definitions are mere descriptions that cannot
account "for the whole of Deity in the Trinity."[66] He clearly affirmed,
however, that "three equal divinities met together in one Deity," and held
the three together in ontological, teleological, and moral unity.[67]

In Brooks's thought, though, the incarnation serves as the major
informant concerning God's nature and character. First, the incarnation confirms God's personality. Christ presents the actual evidence
that God cannot be merely "a method, a law, a habit, a machine," and
proves that God is a Person with "a dear, live, loving nature, all afire
with affection, all radiant with light."[68] Second, the incarnation solidifies
God's immanence, making manifest its eternal reality. In "The Nearness
of God," Brooks raises a rhetorical question about the significance of the

62. Brooks, quoted in Allen, *Life and Letters*, 2:337–38.

63. Ibid., 2:338.

64. Brooks, "New Theism," 157.

65. Ibid.

66. Brooks, quoted in Minyard, "Theology of Phillips Brooks," 119.

67. Ibid., 117. Minyard suspects, however, that Brooks's emphasis on the moral
unity in the Trinity may have found favor among modalist theories.

68. Brooks, "New and Greater Miracle," 38–39.

incarnation and then answers that it reveals the truth that God is forever present:

> What is the meaning of the incarnation? We picture Christ com-
> ing from afar, down through the ranks of angels, down from the
> battlements of heaven; far, far beyond the sun we picture Him
> leaving His eternal seat and "coming down" to save the world.
> Then we picture Christ's departure. Back by the way He came,
> beyond the sun again, once more through the shining hosts, until
> He takes His everlasting seat at the right hand of God. There is
> truth in such pictures. But have we not caught more of the spirit
> of the Incarnation if we think of it, not as the bringing to us of a
> God who had been far away, but as the showing to us of a God
> who had been hidden? It is as if the cloud parted and the tired and
> thirsty traveler saw by his side a brook of clear, sweet water, run-
> ning along close by the road he traveled. Then the cloud closed
> again, but the traveler who had once seen the brook never could
> be faint with thirst again. He must always know where to find it
> and drink of it. Christ was not a God coming out of absence. He
> was the ever-present God, revealing how near He always was.[69]

Brooks stretched this demonstration of God's immanence even to the point of supporting more extreme, romantic notions that creation itself is an expression of the divine life. In Brooks's essay, "The New Theism," the author suggests that the incarnation displays a fundamental unity between God and the world, maintaining that Jesus "gives us reason to believe that there is a real possibility of holding both together, the per- sonality of God and the divine life in the universe."[70]

Not surprisingly, Brooks's "belief in the essential divinity of true man"—proved by the incarnation—also steered his thoughts about God in an anthropocentric direction.[71] He spoke often about the fatherhood of God, the Lord's love for all humanity, and God's activity in the lives of all people. He even conceived the Trinity from the perspective of humanity. In *The Influence of Jesus*, Brooks starts with humanity and moves through the incarnation to arrive at the Trinity, only to conclude that the Trinity itself presents a template of humanity's best social constructions:

> If it be so, as we believe it is, that in the constitution of humanity
> we have the fairest written analogue and picture of the divine

---

69. Brooks, "Nearness of God," 55–56.

70. Brooks, "New Theism," 158.

71. Minyard, "Theology of Phillips Brooks," 121.

existence, then shall we not say that human Christ gave us, in his social thought of God, what we call the doctrine of the Trinity? May it be that only in multiplicity and interior self-relationship can divinity have completed self-consciousness and energy? Surely the reverent and thoughtful eye must see some such meaning when Jesus Himself makes the eternal companionship of the life of Deity the pattern and picture of the best society of souls on earth, and breathes out to His Father these deep and wonderful words, "As Thou, Father, art in me, and I in Thee, that they may all be one in us."[72]

Brooks ultimately portrayed the Trinity as a doctrine about human life. He thus tilted the threefold nature of the Godhead toward the threefold need of humanity:

> The trinity of the soul's needs: first, Causal Deity, then Revealed Deity, then Resident, Regulative Deity. . . . In each the soul will be satisfied with nothing short of divinity, but in each the distinction of offices, of those who shall fulfill its demands, is clearly marked. But yet, notice that the offices, though separate, are not independent; the Causal Will, the Revealing Word, the Regulative Presence—they interfuse each other. The Will issues the Word, the Word reveals the Will. The Permanent Presence develops and perfects the work that the Will originated and the Word declared. Now what have we to answer this threefold yet one need? I confess that I do not know unless the answer lies in that mysterious co-partnership (I do not like the word, that mysterious unity) in which the three equal divinities, Father, Son, and Spirit, are met together in one Deity which we call God. . . . Can I doubt the threeness of the agency? There it is answering the triple need by the threefold supply.[73]

While upholding the bare necessities of an orthodox doctrine of God, Brooks "sailed a course of thought too ambiguous to be definitely charted."[74] With his thoughts on God, he essentially maintained the basic commitments put forward in his incarnation formula—namely, that God is personal and present, and that humans are supremely valuable.

72. Brooks, *Influence of Jesus*, 85.
73. Brooks, quoted in Minyard, "Theology of Phillips Brooks," 112–13.
74. Minyard, "Theology of Phillips Brooks," 120.

The Incarnation as the Essence of Salvation

For Brooks, Christ's incarnation is not only a necessary component of the gospel—it is the gospel. Brooks even spoke boldly of the "redeeming Incarnation."[75] First of all, in his scheme, the incarnation itself has saving power in that Christ is the true man who illustrates what all humanity may become. In "The Manliness of Christ," Brooks constructs the incarnation as the full development of humanity and the pattern for all human life:

> The Incarnation, then, the beginning of the earthly life of Christ, was the fulfillment, the filling full, of a human nature by Divinity. . . . It made the man in whom the miracle occurred, absolutely perfect man. It did not make Him something else than man. If it had done that, all His value as a pattern for humanity . . . would be gone. Whenever He says to men "Follow Me;" "Be like Me," He is declaring that He is man as they are men, that the peculiar Divinity which filled Him, while it carried humanity to its complete development, had not changed that humanity into something which was no longer human. . . . We may pass on then, with this truth clear in our minds, that the Christhood was a true development and not a distortion of humanity.[76]

Therefore, Christ saves people simply by existing as the exemplary, fully developed person to whom all people should aspire.

Second, Brooks contends that the incarnation constitutes salvation because it proves that humans are by nature children of God. Humans indeed sin, and they estrange themselves from God by sinning, but sin has not changed the fundamental truth "that man is eternally the son of God."[77] According to Brooks, "He is ignorant and rebellious—the prodigal child of God, but his ignorance and rebellion never break that first relationship."[78] In fact, in "The Light of the World," Brooks attests that sinfulness comes to light when set against humanity's essential goodness, not depravity:

> Oh, believe me, believe me, my dear friends, you will never know the horror and misery of sin till you know the glory and mystery

75. Brooks, "Fire and the Calf," 62.

76. Brooks, "Manliness of Christ," 256–57.

77. Ibid., 257.

78. Brooks, *Influence of Jesus*, 13–14.

of man. You never can estimate the disaster of an interruption till you know the worth of what it interrupts. You will never understand wickedness by dwelling on the innate depravity of man. You can understand wickedness only by knowing that the very word man means holiness and strength.[79]

Brooks observes, "Man is a son of God on whom the Devil has laid his hand, not a child of the Devil whom God is trying to steal."[80] Consequently, sin exists only parasitically as an "intrusion," meaning that "lies and cruelties and lusts" have no rightful place in human life.[81] In Brooks's thought, sinful behavior fundamentally constitutes a denial of humanity's true identity:

> When we say that we ought to mean that Christ is the only absolutely true man that has ever lived; that all men, just as far as they fall short of Christ, fall short of humanity; that not that Jesus should be sinless, but that every other human being who ever lived should be a sinner, is the real moral wonder of the world.[82]

Since humans remain irrevocable children of God, and because Christ represents the very apex and full potential of humanity, salvation—for Brooks—becomes nothing more than rediscovering and implementing one's true identity as God's child. In *The Influence of Jesus*, Brooks makes his position plain:

> Upon the race and upon the individual, Jesus is always bringing into more and more perfect revelation the certain truth that every man is a child of God. This is the sum of the work of the Incarnation. . . .
> The opening life of Jesus was full of his consciousness that he was the Son of God. The ambition of which his soul was full was the desire to let men know that they, too, were the sons of God, and to rescue them into the full enjoyment of their sonship.[83]

Brooks's vision of salvation simplifies Christianity in such a way that eliminates any need for supernatural transformation. In "The Light of the World," Brooks claims that

---

79. Brooks, "Light of the World," 21–22.
80. Ibid., 9.
81. Brooks, quoted in Minyard, "Theology of Phillips Brooks," 132.
82. Brooks, "Transfiguration of Christ," 128.
83. Brooks, *Influence of Jesus*, 12, 124.

> the Christian is nothing but the true man. . . . The Christian
> graces are nothing but the natural virtues held up to the light of
> Christ. They are made of the same stuff; they are lifted along the
> same lines, but they have found their pinnacle. They have caught
> the illumination which their souls desire. Manliness has not been
> changed into Godliness; it has fulfilled itself in Godliness.[84]

In due course, then, the "awakening of the spiritual element in any man
is just his coming to know and act on the knowledge that he is a child
of God."[85]

Predictably, the spiritual awakening of which Brooks speaks follows an incarnational pattern. In his thought, the union of the divine
and human natures in Christ occurred ontologically, but also—and
more importantly—on a moral plane. Brooks proclaims, "God's will and
Christ's obedience! Here is the perfect mutualness . . . in harmony of will
and obedience they are absolutely one."[86] As a result, spiritual awakening
happens in humans when they repeat this same moral union with God:

> And so when the possession of the soul by Christ is called the
> "New Birth," one of the meanings of that name is this, that then
> there is a reassertion of personality, and the soul which had lost
> itself in the slavery of the multitude finds itself again in the obe-
> dience of Christ. . . .
>
> Out of his sin, out of the bad, base, cowardly acts which are
> truly his, out of the weak and wretched passages of his life which
> it makes him ashamed to remember, but which he forces himself
> to recollect and own, out of these he gathers the consciousness of
> a self all astray with self-will which he then brings to Christ and
> offers in submission and obedience to His perfect will.[87]

Brooks explains that "the Incarnation of God in Jesus is repeated and
fulfilled in the occupation of a faithful and obedient humanity by God,
that is the promised salvation of the world."[88]

---

84. Brooks, "Light of the World," 8–9.
85. Brooks, "Spiritual Man," 300.
86. Brooks, "Knowledge of God," 290–91.
87. Brooks, "Fire and the Calf," 62–63.
88. Brooks, "Why Could We Not Cast Him Out?" 193.

Evaluation

Every facet of Brooks's theology orbits around the axis formed between the two poles of Christ's incarnation and humanity's eternal sonship. On the one hand, the incarnation serves a preventive role in keeping his thoughts from sliding into transcendentalism or other forms of monism. On the other hand, the incarnation plays a positive role in enabling him to promote his main romantic conviction that humans are—immutably— children of God. His convictions concerning revelation, truth, God, and salvation all follow suit, each working through the incarnation and humanity up to the Creator. In Brooks's plan, truth becomes unified with personality; God reflects the image of humanity; and salvation occurs by progress in morality.

Brooks's system forces the neglect—even the negation—of two fundamental Christian doctrines. First, original sin has no place in a theological structure that disallows the biblical claim that humans are "by nature children of wrath" (Eph 2:3). He emphatically denied the doctrine, asking in one sermon, "Well, what do we mean by 'original sin'? Not surely that each being comes into the world guilty, already bearing the burden of responsible sin." For him, such a doctrine is "horrible theology" that "nobody holds to-day."[89] Second, his system requires an extreme weakening of the atonement. Brooks did not dismiss the atonement completely, but he set aside traditional substitutionary formulations to focus more intently on the incarnation, which for him was the divine affirmation of humanity's inherent and eternal worth.[90] Charles McIlvaine insightfully detected the theological negligence caused by placing such an inordinate priority on the incarnation, and correctly proclaimed the dangers of this imbalance:

> You may preach the incarnation of Christ in all its truth as a separate event, and yet in great error as regards its relation to other events, making it so unduly prominent that His death shall be made to appear comparatively subordinate and unessential,—the means exalted above the end,—the preparation of the body of Christ for sacrifice being made of more importance and more effective in our salvation, than His offering of that body on the cross.[91]

---

89. Brooks, "Mystery of Iniquity," 5–6.
90. Harp, *Brahmin Prophet*, 138.
91. McIlvaine, *Work of Preaching Christ*, 17–18.

David Wells insists, "The Incarnation can only be understood aright when we see it within God's overarching purposes of salvation."[92] Brooks—being so highly influenced by, and dedicated to, his romantic anthropology—not only misunderstood the incarnation, but also misapplied it in a way that misconstrues the fundamental evangelical concept of sinners' salvation by grace through faith in Jesus Christ. Several New Testament passages that deal particularly with the matter of salvation cannot—without a certain level of exegetical dishonesty—be considered apart from original sin and substitutionary atonement:

> But now apart from the Law the righteousness of God has been manifested, being witnessed by the Law and the Prophets, even the righteousness of God through faith in Jesus Christ for all those who believe; for there is no distinction; for all have sinned and fall short of the glory of God, being justified as a gift by His grace through the redemption which is in Christ Jesus; whom God displayed publicly as a propitiation in His blood through faith (Rom 3:21–25a).

> He made Him who knew no sin to be sin on our behalf, so that we might become the righteousness of God in Him (2 Cor 5:21).

> For Christ also died for sins once for all, the just for the unjust, so that He might bring us to God, having been put to death in the flesh, but made alive in the spirit (1 Pet 3:18).

> And if anyone sins, we have an Advocate with the Father, Jesus Christ the righteous; and He Himself is the propitiation for our sins; and not for ours only, but for those of the whole world (1 John 2:1b-2).

In sum, it appears that Brooks, although he believed himself to be preaching the Christian gospel, actually centered upon just one gospel element—Christ's incarnation. In fact, he generalized and universalized the incarnation in support of an anthropocentric agenda, which had much more kinship with romanticism than it did with evangelical Christianity.

---

92. Wells, *Person of Christ*, 175.

THE INCARNATIONAL SHAPE OF BROOKS'S
DEFINITION OF PREACHING

No better illustration of Phillips Brooks's preaching definition exists than the one displayed by his memorial statue outside Trinity Church in Copley Square, Boston. Brooks—with his imposing physique—stands beside, and slightly in front of, his pulpit; his entire body is fully engaged in proclamation. His right arm is raised in a declarative gesture, and his left hand grips the front of the lectern. Behind him hovers a mystical and shrouded Christ figure, whose right hand rests on Brooks's left shoulder. Brooks remarks, in his *Lectures on Preaching*, that "Christian ministry is not the mere practice of a set of rules and precedents, but is a broad, free, fresh meeting of a man with men, in such close contact that the Christ who has entered into his life may, through his, enter into theirs."[93] Christ's incarnation, as the center of Brooks's theology, additionally forms the paradigm for his definition of preaching as "truth through personality." The above demonstration of the centrality of the doctrine in his theology, indeed, serves as prolegomena to the exposition of his preaching definition.

Each of Brooks's eight lectures unpacks some aspect of the preaching definition that the first lecture offers:

> What, then, is preaching, of which we are to speak? It is not hard to find a definition. Preaching is the communication of truth by man to man. It has in it two essential elements, truth and personality. Neither of those can it spare and still be preaching. . . . [P]reaching is the bringing of truth through personality.[94]

As the *Lectures* cover topics like the preacher's personality and work, the concept and preparation of a sermon, the role of the congregation and culture, and the supreme value of humanity, they incessantly depend on the incarnational tenets of Brooks's theology. The phrase itself, "truth through personality," is brief and compact but—as he unfolds its intended meaning in his *Lectures*—it appears essentially as a restatement of his formulation and application of the incarnation, only in homiletical terms.

93. Brooks, *Lectures*, 106.

94. Ibid., 5. The lectures, in order, are titled "The Two Elements in Preaching," "The Preacher Himself," "The Preacher in His Work," "The Idea of the Sermon," "The Making of the Sermon," "The Congregation," "The Ministry for Our Age," and "The Value of the Human Soul."

The Personality of Truth

Prior to functioning as homiletical procedure, "truth through person-ality" first embraces a theory of truth, and Brooks's incarnational and anthropocentric notion of truth naturally assumes full residence in his definition. Throughout the *Lectures,* he noticeably maintains an ex-tremely close relationship between truth and personality, and at times nearly folds the two completely together. According to the first lecture, "Truth is preeminently personal," and the truest statement of the gospel "is not in dogma but in personal life."[95] While Brooks calls truth the "fixed and stable" component, to which personality provides a "varying and growing" element,[96] he nonetheless refuses to sever one from the other. In his view, it is impossible to consider truth "wholly by itself" because "personalness will cling to it."[97] In fact, Brooks deals with the New Testament distinction between the message and the messenger by holding them in unity:

> There are two aspects of the minister's work, which we are con-stantly meeting in the New Testament. They are really embodied in two words, one of which is "message," and the other is "witness." "This is the message which we have heard of Him and declare to you," says St. John in his first Epistle. "We are His witnesses of these things," says St. Peter before the Council at Jerusalem. In these two words together, I think, we have the fundamental con-cept of the matter of all Christian preaching. It is to be a message given to us for transmission, but yet a message which we cannot transmit until it has entered into our own experience, and we can give our own testimony of its spiritual power.[98]

Brooks eventually goes so far as to say that the preacher's "message *is* his witness," and he holds that, out of this union, preaching finds "all the authority and independence of assured truth, and yet all the appeal and convincingness of personal belief."[99] Brooks contends that his personal notion of truth guards preaching from dissolving into strictly objective

95. Ibid., 7.

96. Ibid., 28.

97. Ibid., 14.

98. Ibid. On this point, Brooks notably contradicts two evangelical Episcopal preaching exemplars of his day, Charles McIlvaine and Stephen Tyng, who maintained the "tidy distinction between subject and object." Harp, *Brahmin Prophet,* 118.

99. Brooks, *Lectures,* 15, 18. Emphasis mine.

"criticism" or impersonal "mechanism."[100] In effect, he ultimately believes the "personalness" of truth constitutes the main factor that necessitates preaching and renders it irreplaceable. Brooks argues, "Nothing can ever take its place because of the personal element that is in it."[101]

In the fourth lecture, "The Idea of the Sermon," he returns to the matter of homiletical authority and insists that the "absolute authority of the message is in some degree qualified" because "the messenger must mingle himself with the message."[102] According to him, it is simply a fact that "speculations, personal opinions, prejudices . . . must attach themselves to any live man's utterance of the truth."[103] For this reason, Brooks claims that a preacher should—while preaching—delineate a distinction between "God's truth" and "what I think."[104] His intimate connection between truth and personality, however, makes the distinction impossible. He continues in the same lecture,

> I cannot do my duty of making Christ plain unless I tell them of Him all the richness that I know. I must keep nothing back. All that has come to me about Him from His Word, all that has grown clear to me about His nature or His methods by my inward or outward experience, all that He has told me of Himself, becomes part of the message that I must tell to those men whom He has sent me to call home to Himself. I will do this in its fullness. And this is the preaching of doctrine, positive, distinct, characteristic Christian Truth.[105]

Brooks seemingly senses the need to separate truth from personality, but his extremely personal concept of truth forces the effort to fail.

Brooks addresses the Bible's place within his framework of truth in his fifth lecture, "The Making of the Sermon." He admits that the "power of a sermon style corresponds very largely with the question about the inspiration of the Scriptures," and proceeds to offer various theories pertaining to whether the locus of inspiration lies in the words themselves, in the biblical authors, or in the "things they wrote about."[106] Brooks

---

100. Ibid., 19.
101. Ibid., 11.
102. Ibid., 122.
103. Ibid., 123.
104. Ibid., 124.
105. Ibid., 128.
106. Ibid., 148–49.

thinks that "all three ideas are true in their degrees," but urges preachers to look to the "deepest truth in the matter," which, he claims, is character. Brooks contends, "He who aspires to the strength of truth and character will be a stronger man than he who tries to prevail by the finish and completeness of his language."[107] For him, the rise of biblical criticism—far from undermining the preaching task—actually enhances the Bible's role because it gives preachers a vision of the deeper, character-filled meaning of Scripture. The "change in the way of considering the Bible . . . has led men to desire an entrance into the heart and spirit of the Bible," instead of merely "weighing text against text."[108]

Immediately beneath the surface of Brooks's statements about the authority of preaching and use of Scripture resides his conviction that revelation occurs incarnationally within human personalities. While encouraging the preacher to find "your truth" in a biblical text and warning against drawing out of a text "a meaning which you know is not there,"[109] he nonetheless places the true power of preaching neither in the text nor in any external authority, but in the person of the preacher. Thus, the "real question about a sermon" is if "the discourse sprang freshly from your heart and mind."[110] Brooks asserts,

> [T]he real power of your oratory must be your own intelligent delight in what you are doing. Let your pulpit be to you what his studio is to the artist, or his courtroom to the lawyer, or his laboratory to the chemist, or the broad field with its bugles and banners to the soldier; only far more sacredly let your pulpit be this to you, and you have the power which is to all rules what the soul is to the body. You have the enthusiasm which is the breath of life.[111]

With his personal conception of truth and power in view, it comes as no surprise that Brooks prioritizes choosing a topic over selecting a biblical text.[112] Truth is essentially personal for him, and Scripture—with character at its core—serves to support that which God has revealed in the person of the preacher.

---

107. Ibid., 149.
108. Ibid., 160–61.
109. Ibid., 163.
110. Ibid., 172.
111. Ibid., 179.
112. Ibid., 149.

Truth Mediated through Personality

At its heart, "truth through personality" exists as a statement concerning agency. For Brooks, truth—particularly Christian truth—can be communicated only by means of personality in a manner directly analogous to the incarnation. He makes this fundamental idea quite clear in the first lecture, "The Two Elements in Preaching":

> Preaching is the communication of truth by man to men. The truest truth, the most authoritative statement of God's will, communicated in any other way than through the personality of brother man to men is not preached truth. . . . And preaching is the bringing of truth through personality. . . .
>
> If we go back to the beginning of the Christian ministry we can see how distinctly and deliberately Jesus chose this method of extending the knowledge of Himself throughout the world. Other methods no doubt were open to Him, but He deliberately selected this. He taught this truth to a few men and then He said, "Now go and tell that truth to other men." . . .
>
> This was the method by which Christ chose that His Gospel should spread through the world. It was a method that might have been applied to the dissemination of any truth, but we can see why it was especially adapted to the truth of Christianity. . . . Christianity is Christ; and we can easily understand how a truth which is of such peculiar character that a person can stand forth and say of it, "I am the Truth," must always be best conveyed through, must indeed be almost incapable of being perfectly conveyed except through personality. . . . There seems to be some such meaning as this in the words of Jesus when He said to His disciples, "As my Father has sent me into the world even so I have sent you into the world." It was the continuation, out to the minutest ramifications of the new system of influence, of that personal method which the Incarnation itself had involved.[113]

Brooks mentions this central theme repeatedly throughout the *Lectures*— especially in the fourth lecture, "The Idea of the Sermon," and the fifth lecture, "The Making of the Sermon."

Preaching defined as "truth through personality" places a remarkable level of responsibility on the preacher in three distinct areas. First of all, "truth through personality" requires the preparation of the preacher's character. In the *Lectures*, Brooks presents preaching as the opening of a

---

113. Ibid., 5–7.

personality to God's truth on one side, and to humanity on the other. He further explains that this is the way Jesus cultivated the apostles:

> If He gave them the power of working miracles, the miracles themselves were not the final purpose for which He gave it. The power of miracle was, as it were, a divine fire pervading the Apostle's being and opening his individuality on either side; making it more open God-wards by the sense of awful privilege, making it more open man-wards by the impressiveness and the helpfulness with which it was clothed. Everything that was peculiar in Christ's treatment of those men was merely part of the process by which the Master prepared their personality to be a fit medium for the communication of His Word. When His treatment of them was complete, they stood fused like glass, and able to take God's truth in perfectly on one side and send it out perfectly on the other side of their transparent natures.[114]

Consequently, preaching's initial principle is the "making of a man."[115] According to Brooks, "It must be nothing less than the kneading and tempering of a man's whole nature till it becomes of such a consistency and quality as to be capable of transmission." In the second lecture, "The Preacher Himself," Brooks alleges that a preacher must possess piety, a desire to send truth abroad, hopefulness, physical stamina, and a certain indescribable quality that renders one a "born preacher."[116] Each of these qualifications exists in degrees and is "capable of culture."[117] Brooks places the greatest emphasis on piety, though, because "only fire kindles fire," and he closes the discussion with an assertion that true training largely involves the formation of character. Once a qualified preacher finds himself preaching, Brooks echoes similar themes in ascertaining what "elements of personal power . . . will make him successful," focusing on "the supreme importance of character."[118]

As a second responsibility, "truth through personality" necessitates that a preacher embody the truth he preaches. Embodiment seems to be a necessary corollary of Brooks's idea of truth, but he nonetheless highlights it in his *Lectures*. In reality, the preacher's embodiment of truth

---

114. Ibid., 6–7.
115. Ibid., 9.
116. Ibid., 38–41.
117. Ibid., 42.
118. Ibid., 38, 43–45, 49.

comprises the core of sermon content and forms his actual definition of the term "doctrine." In the second lecture, Brooks states,

> [T]he minister's preparation of character for his work involves something more intimate than the accumulation of knowledge. The knowledge which comes into him meets in him the intention of preaching, and, touched by that, undergoes a transformation. It is changed into doctrine. Doctrine means this,—truth considered with its reference to its being taught. . . . [T]he mere student preparing to be a preacher cannot learn truth as the mere student of theology for its own sake might do. He always feels it reaching out through him to the people to whom he is some day to carry it. He cannot get rid of this consciousness.[119]

On a practical level, this responsibility to embody truth leads Brooks to caution preachers about delivering "old sermons" and against being overtly autobiographical. In regard to preaching old sermons, he continues,

> It is not good. A new sermon, fresh from the brain, has always a life in it which an old sermon, though better in itself, must lack. The trouble is in the prominence of that personal element in preaching of which I spoke in my first lecture. . . . You may reproduce the paper but you cannot reproduce the man, and the sermon was man and paper together.[120]

As for employing autobiographical elements in preaching, Brooks encourages restraint and stresses that such self-control does not limit or hinder embodiment.

> It is not the man who forces the events of his life on you who most puts the spirit of his life into you. The most unreserved men are not the most influential. A reserved man who cares for truth, and cares that his brethren should know the truth, who therefore is always holding back the mere envelope of accident and circumstance in which the truth has embodied itself to him, and yet sending for the truth with all the clearness and force which it has gathered for him from that embodiment, he is the best preacher, as everywhere he is the most influential man.[121]

119. Ibid., 46.
120. Ibid., 103.
121. Ibid., 120.

Reciprocally and ultimately, as a preacher embodies truth, the sermon "embodies and declares" the preacher. "I think that a man's best sermon is the best utterance of his life. . . . If it really is God's message through him, it brings him out in a way that no other experience of his life has power to do."[122] As a result, in Brooks's model, truth conquers precisely as it is embodied in a person of pure character.[123]

Transmission—or even transfusion—of truth makes up the third and decisive responsibility issued to preachers by "truth through personality." In the opening lecture, Brooks delineates the difference between truth coming "through" and merely coming "over" a preacher. He purports,

> The truth must come really through the person, not merely over his lips, not merely into his understanding and out through his pen. It must come through his character, his affections, his whole intellectual and moral being. It must come genuinely through him. I think that, granting equal intelligence and study, here is the great difference which we feel between two preachers of the Word. The Gospel has come *over* one of them and reaches us tinged and flavored with his superficial characteristics, belittled with his littleness. The Gospel has come *through* the other, and we receive it impressed and winged with all the earnestness and strength that there is in him. In the first case the man has been but a printing machine or a trumpet. In the other case he has been a true man and real messenger of God.[124]

Brooks observes in the fifth lecture that this dynamic distinguishes authentic preaching from trite sermonizing:

> The sermon is truth and man together; it is the truth brought through the man. The personal element is essential. Now the truth which the preacher has gathered on Friday for the sermon which he preaches on Sunday has come across the man, but it has not come through the man. It has never been wrought into his experience. It comes weighted and winged with none of his personal life. If it is true, it is a book's truth, not a man's truth that we get. It does not make a full, real sermon.[125]

---

122. Ibid., 135.
123. Ibid., 50.
124. Ibid., 8.
125. Ibid., 159.

This authenticity that Brooks requires—truth genuinely coming through personality—represents more than the public display of embodiment. For him, preaching cannot be an art form that contains intrinsic aesthetic value.[126] Rather, as the phrase "truth through personality" implies, his concept of preaching is—fundamentally—a method of transferring, and even infusing, truth from one to another. "There is nothing which a sermon ought to be," Brooks maintains in the fourth lecture, "except a fit medium of truth to men."[127] Alexander Allen accurately and lucidly captures the whole intent of Brooks's lectures when he states, "The leading idea is that truth and moral efficiency in the will are contagious, and pass from man to man through the medium of personality."[128]

Personality Formed by Personal Truth

Any definition of preaching remains incomplete without a clear teleology, and Brooks's "truth through personality"—as a utilitarian homiletic—certainly has its goal. According to him, "A sermon exists in and for its purpose. That purpose is the persuading and moving of men's souls."[129] The personal embodiment of personal truth, transferred from one to another by means of personality, aims toward "what in the largest extent of those great words might be described as *saving souls*."[130] After declaring this persuasive and salvific objective, however, Brooks swings sharply toward his anthropocentric application of the incarnation in his teleology. In the third lecture, he proposes,

> The life of Jesus Christ was radical. . . . It claimed men's noblest and freest action. We, if we are His ministers, must bring the heroic into the unheroic life of men, demanding of them truth, breadth, bravery, self-sacrifice, the freedom from conventionalities and an elevation to high standards of thought and life. We must bring men's life up to Him and not bring Him down to men's life. This is the Christian pastor's privilege and duty.
>
> It seems to me that a large part of the troubles and mistakes of our pastoral life come from our having too high an estimate of men's present condition and too low an estimate of their possibil-

126. Ibid., 109–11.
127. Ibid., 114.
128. Allen, *Life and Letters*, 2:305.
129. Brooks, *Lectures*, 110.
130. Ibid., 112.

ity. If this be true, then what we need to make us better pastors is more of the Gospel which reveals at once man's imperfect condition and his infinite hope. Jesus was the perfect pastor in the way in which He showed men what they were and what they might become. . . . Let that be the model of our pastorship.[131]

Throughout the *Lectures*, Brooks echoes his anthropological commitments, making statements that refer to the awakening of "the stronger nature in man," the natural attraction to a "higher life," the reality that every heart has the "power of appreciating genuine spiritual truth," and the "essential religiousness of man."[132]

Brooks saves his thoughts on the ultimate motive for preaching for the final lecture, "The Value of the Human Soul," in which he reveals with force:

There is a power which lies at the center of all success in preaching, and whose influence reaches out to the circumference, and is essential everywhere. . . . Without this power preaching is almost sure to become either a struggle of ambition or a burden of routine. With it preaching is an ever fresh delight. The power is the value of the human soul, felt by the preacher, and inspiring all his work. The power of that motive has been assumed in all that I have said to you.[133]

Brooks's eighth lecture runs replete with his Christianized romantic anthropology as he affirms that "man is full of the suggestion of God," and the "Christliness" that "fills the souls of all God's children."[134] Consequent to and consistent with these notions, a sermon becomes an effort "sacrificed to the soul," and preaching mainly concerns the attainment of "personal perfection."[135]

Brooks ultimately identifies "preaching Christ" as the subject of preaching, yet immediately inquires:

But what is Christ? "The saving power of the world," we say. Where is His power, then, to reach? Wherever men are wrong;

131. Ibid., 81.
132. Ibid., 79, 201, 241, 230.
133. Ibid., 255–56.
134. Ibid., 259, 273.
135. Ibid., 268, 261.

wherever men are capable of being better; wherever His authority and love can make them better.[136]

Brooks's heightened, romantic anthropology—supported by a humanistic version of the incarnation—thus steers his homiletic distinctly toward
the goal of character formation, not to spiritual transformation.

CONCLUSION

The connections between a preacher's theology and his homiletical theory run wide and deep. Fred Craddock rightly comments, "When a man
preaches, his method of communication, the movement of his sermon,
reflects his hermeneutical principles, his view of the authority of Scripture
. . . and especially his doctrine of man. . . . How one communicates is
a theological commentary on this minister's view of the ministry, the
church, the Word of God, sin, salvation, faith, works, love, and hope."[137]
Christ's incarnation, formulated and applied in a distinctly anthropocentric manner, forms the axis of Brooks's theology. In his thought, the
doctrine serves as the model for anthropology, the source of revelation
and truth, the informant for the doctrine of God, and the essence of salvation. Brooks's singular focus on the incarnation greatly simplifies his
concept of Christianity, rendering traditional doctrines—such as original sin and substitutionary atonement—unnecessary and even offensive.
"We have those things which seemed essential to Christianity again and
again shown to be only incidental to Christianity," he explains. "We have
seen how absolutely simple essential Christianity is."[138]

The incarnation equally dominates and shapes his preaching definition. "Truth through personality" is a succinct phrase that can be construed in multiple ways but, in Brooks's scheme, it stands as a statement
regarding the personal nature of truth; the incarnational means of trans-
mitting truth; and the development of truth within individuals for the
purpose of identity realization (as a natural child of God) and character
formation. He clearly constructs in the *Lectures* a homiletical theory
that restates and supports his main theological commitments—namely,
that Christ's incarnation procures an exalted perspective of humanity.
Consequently, preaching becomes chiefly concerned with human affir-

---

136. Ibid., 136.
137. Craddock, *As One without Authority*, 44.
138. Brooks, *Essays and Addresses*, 148.

mation and character-building. Of all Brooks's biographers and analysts, only Raymond Albright grasps and expresses this essential theological structure of Brooks's definition. He comments,

> The heart of his lectures is discerned only when the essence of the final one on "The Value of the Human Soul" is allowed to penetrate all the others. . . .
>
> Just as his chief motivation for the ministry lay in his high valuation of the human soul so Brooks declared that his supreme duty as a minister was to permit the truth of God to manifest itself through his own life and soul. Side by side these ideas had been maturing in Brooks's mind . . . demanding his consideration.[139]

Because Brooks's incarnational and anthropocentric theology remains explicitly present within "truth through personality," his preaching definition necessarily represents a significant departure from traditional evangelical homiletics. Gillis Harp maintains that Brooks aimed to "redefine substantially the meaning of preaching in modern American Protestantism," and that he was "uniquely suited" to facilitate the "freeing" of homiletics from the constraints of abstract doctrinal constructs.[140] Without any real obligation to creedal theology or even to the biblical text, the person of the preacher—in Brooks's model—surmounts the locus of authority. Ozora Davis, writing in 1926, observes the ongoing effect of Brooks's definition into the early part of the twentieth century:

> The emancipation of the American pulpit from this bondage was well under way by the beginning of the century; but it was far from completed. It is safe to say that the most influential preachers today are those who have broken from the dogmatic fetters and are taking "the direct look" at life. The actual experience of living men and women in their experiment with the principles of Jesus as a way of living furnishes the most and the best of the material that is found in the sermons of today.[141]

The fact that Brooks's definition played a major role in liberating preaching from doctrinal content should trouble evangelicals, especially considering that evangelicalism is—after all—the conviction that Christianity requires certain essential doctrines. He ignored or denied both theologically and homiletically some of these doctrines, like sub-

---

139. Albright, *Focus on Infinity*, 188.

140. Harp, *Brahmin Prophet*, 117, 128.

141. Davis, "A Quarter-Century," 140–41.

stitutionary atonement and supernatural conversion. If Brooks's definition of preaching as "truth through personality" retains any sustained
value for evangelical preaching—if it is "the imperishable idea about
preaching"[142]—then it must be assessed in light of evangelical convictions and reconstructed in a way that includes evangelical doctrines.

142. Turnbull, *From the Close of the Nineteenth Century*, 111.

4

Out of Bounds

HIGHLIGHTING THE PREVALENT INFLUENCE of romanticism on Phillips Brooks and identifying the incarnational and anthropocentric shape of his theology help evangelicals avoid a common error: believing that "truth through personality" means something that he never intended. Bryan Chapell's contention that the concept "reflects biblical principle" illustrates the mistake—his blunder made evident by Brooks's dismissive stance concerning the Bible and strangely man-centered twist on the incarnation.[1] Wayne McDill commits a similar gaffe when he acknowledges the deficiencies of Brooks's theology, but still endorses his definition of preaching.[2] If Brooks built his preaching definition upon philosophical commitments and theological constructs that fall outside the bounds of evangelical Christianity, then—by necessity—the definition itself fails as a useful boundary for evangelical preaching. In order to salvage the concept and reconstruct it in an evangelical manner, though, it remains important to specify the failures of Brooks's construction of "truth through personality"—a task this chapter undertakes.

The most natural way to identify the deficiencies in Brooks's preaching definition occurs by assessing the concept along the same categories it presents: a conviction about the nature of truth, an incarnational notion of the preacher himself, and a character-driven model of persuasion. This chapter reviews each of these topics in the order of four steps. First, it traces the lines of thought in Brooks's definition through their historical and contemporary development. Second, it evaluates these concepts in light of biblical data and traditional evangelical doctrines. Third, it reestablishes theological foundations for evangelical preaching. Fourth, it precisely pinpoints the defects of "truth through personality."

1. Chapell, *Christ-Centered Preaching*, 36.
2. McDill, *Moment of Truth*, 23.

Delineating the problems of his definition in this chapter sets the stage for the reconstructive work that follows in the next chapter.

PROPOSITIONAL REVELATION AND THE TROUBLE FOR "TRUTH THROUGH PERSONALITY"

Unmistakably, every homiletical theory flows from a particular concept of revelation. Whether revelation is conceived as proposition, person, or poetry, a similar approach to Scripture follows, and a consistent style of preaching emerges.[3] As maintained in previous chapters, Brooks's exceptionally personal approach to preaching rests upon his equally personal notions of revelation and truth. In his scheme, God's truth arises within personalities in a manner that is directly analogous to Christ's incarnation. Truth has an internal, not an external, existence. The incarnation, therefore—as the source and mode of revelation—furnishes the ground, model, and content of preaching.[4] In this manner, Brooks separated internal truth from external doctrine and built a preaching model in which the dynamics of personality far overshadow any propositional substance.[5]

The Trend toward Nonpropositional Revelation

Brooks's claim that Christianity is not "a scheme of truth to be believed," but "a person to be believed in,"[6] illustrates an important link between romantic thought and a major theological trend that took hold in the twentieth century. As Kantian epistemology provided the functional foundation for romanticism and its escape from Enlightenment methodologies, the impasse between the noumenal and the phenomenal eventually bore fruit in "making theology less about confident doctrinal assertions and more about socioethical concerns."[7] As a result, the "personality of Jesus"—instead of specific propositions concerning Jesus—came to form the dominant concept of revelation, further facilitating the slide of Protestantism into liberalism.[8] Even Karl Barth, who famously attempted

---

3. Adam, *Speaking God's Words*, 92.

4. Brooks, *Lectures*, 7, 85, 260.

5. Brooks, "Pulpit and Popular Skepticism," 73; idem, "Heresy," 8; idem, *Lectures*, 149, 160–61.

6. Brooks, "Pulpit and Popular Skepticism," 74.

7. Thornbury, "Prolegomena," 39–40.

8. McLoughlin, "Introduction," 14, 20.

to rescue Christianity from both liberalism and the Enlightenment, would not fully assert the propositional form of revelation. For him, revelation is an "occasional in-breaking of the divine into history," making the Bible "not itself revelation, but only . . . the witness to it." No more than "Jesus Christ" is "revelation itself."[9] Other significant theologians adopted the same train of thought. In his Gifford Lectures, which were offered at the University of Glasgow in the early 1930s, William Temple remarks, "Revelation is not truth concerning God but the living God Himself."[10] On the whole, during the first half of the twentieth century, the Kantian legacy rendered a widespread theological view that disallowed the possibility of supernatural revelation taking place in the form of human language.[11] Even the midcentury movement toward narrative theology—with its frustration over Enlightenment-driven, historical-critical methods—could not avoid the Kantian divide. Narrative theologians, such as Hans Frei and Paul Ricoeur, generally affirmed the "truth" of the Bible, but only in terms of practicality and effect, and not in terms of metaphysical or historical facts.[12] Donald Bloesch observes, "Here one can discern the influence of Kant's claim that practical reason rather than theoretical reason places us in contact with reality."[13] Bloesch's criticism, however, seems hypocritical considering the Kantian dichotomy present in his own revelation formula:

> The bane of much of modern evangelicalism is rationalism which presupposes that the Word of God is directly available to human reason. It is fashionable to refer to the biblical revelation as propositional. . . . At the same time we must not infer that the propositional statements in the Bible are themselves revealed.[14]

In short, the contemporary resistance to propositional revelation can be traced back through narrative theology, neoorthodoxy, and romanticism, and ultimately to Kant's idealist epistemology.

---

9. Ibid., 42; Barth, *CD* 1/2: 463, 168.

10. Temple, *Nature, Man, and God*, 322.

11. Thornbury, "Prolegomena," 42. See also Henry, *God, Revelation, and Authority*, 1:389–91.

12. Bloesch, *Holy Scripture*, 209.

13. Ibid.

14. Bloesch, *Essentials*, 1:75–76.

Any significant shift in theology typically precipitates a swing in homiletics.[15] In due course, Fred Craddock's 1971 book, *As One without Authority,* fully applied a personal, experiential model of revelation to the task of preaching. In his theory, the goal of preaching is not depositing biblical information or controlling a specific response, but leading the listeners to experience the Word of God and allowing them to respond on their own.[16] Craddock comments, "The sole purpose is to engage the hearer in the pursuit of an issue or an idea so that he will think his own thoughts and experience his own feelings in the presence of Christ and in the light of the Gospel."[17] Craddock's book essentially birthed what became known as the New Homiletic—a paradigm for preaching that has the experience of the listener as its main focus.[18]

With the theological and homiletical movements of the twentieth century in view, Brooks appears to be a man ahead of his time—a seminal demonstration of the profound influence of romanticism on American Protestant Christianity.[19] His preaching definition and the revelatory themes that inform it remarkably foreshadow subsequent theological and homiletical trends. Indeed, he emphatically expressed his belief in language stunningly similar to later theologians—that "if the true revelation of God is in Christ, the Bible is not properly a revelation, but the History of a Revelation. This is not only a Fact but a necessity, for a Person cannot be revealed in a Book, but must find revelation, if at all, in a Person."[20] Consequently, for him, the preeminently personal nature of truth required preaching to be more an "expression of personal life" than a statement of propositions.[21] Brooks even stressed concern for the audience in a way that found full expression in Craddock's work. In the *Lectures on Preaching,* Brooks says, "The main question about sermons is whether they feel their hearers."[22]

---

15. See Allen, "A Tale of Two Roads," 498.

16. Craddock, *As One without Authority,* 157.

17. Ibid., 39.

18. Reid et al., "Preaching as the Creation of an Experience," 1; Reid, "Postmodernism," 7–8.

19. Harp, *Brahmin Prophet,* 208.

20. Brooks, quoted in Allen, *Life and Letters,* 2:352.

21. Ibid., 3:94–95; Brooks, *Lectures,* 7.

22. Brooks, *Lectures,* 172.

The Inadequacy of Nonpropositional Revelation for Preaching

Assessing the adequacy of Brooks's revelatory model for preaching necessitates an evaluation of the "aversion to the words of God, and to
the idea that God speaks" found in modern theology.[23] Peter Adam, in
Speaking God's Words: A Practical Theology of Preaching, emphasizes
both the error and motive of the nonpropositional approach. According
to him, the error of excluding words from God's self-revelation is that of
a false dichotomy:

> My argument is that this viewpoint separates what is seen as be-
> ing together in Scripture. I am not arguing that speaking is the
> only form of revelation; but in the Bible the God who is present
> to act, to give signs of his presence, and to disclose himself, is
> also the God who speaks. Take, for example, the revelation of
> God at Mount Sinai. God has come down to rescue his people
> from the land of the Egyptians (Exod 3:8), and now descends to
> the top of Mount Sinai (Exod 19:20). God is present. While the
> people may not see God, Moses and the elders see the God of
> Israel (Exod 19:21; 24:10). God is seen. There are visible signs of
> his presence: thunder and lightning, thick cloud, trumpet blast,
> smoke and fire (Exod 19:16–19). All these are part of the rev-
> elation, but it is obvious that the main content of the revelation
> comes in words; it is by God's words that Moses knows to come
> near, and by God's speaking that the Ten Words are given and
> the covenant explained. The words of God are not only spoken
> but written down, and the name and glory of God are revealed in
> the word proclaimed by the Lord as he passes by Moses. . . . The
> Bible's assumption is that part of God's self-revelation includes
> his speaking.[24]

John Stott agrees:

> The modern theological tendency is to lay much emphasis on the
> historical activity of God and to deny that he has spoken; to say
> that God's self-revelation has been in deeds not words, personal
> not propositional; and in fact to insist that the redemption is it-
> self the revelation. But this is a false distinction, which Scripture
> itself does not envisage.[25]

---

23. Adam, *Speaking God's Words,* 18.
24. Ibid.
25. Stott, *Between Two Worlds,* 95.

The Bible prevents itself from being conceived as a mere record of revelation or as a witness to revelation. Scripture indeed supports the authenticity of its words as God's words. D. Martyn Lloyd-Jones counts 3,808 occurrences of the phrases "the Lord said," "the Lord spoke," and "the word of the Lord came" in the Old Testament alone, offering ample evidence that the Bible claims to speak the words of God.[26] In the New Testament, Jesus clearly affirms the divine origin of Scripture (Matt 4:4; 19:4–5), as do the apostles (Acts 1:16; 2:16–17). Perhaps no verse in the Bible paints the picture more clearly than does 2 Timothy 3:16. Paul writes, "All Scripture is God-breathed." Thomas Lea and Hayne Griffin labor to demonstrate in their commentary that, in this verse, (1) the term γραφὴ refers to the entire Old Testament; (2) Paul makes a collective reference to Scripture; (3) the translation "all Scripture is inspired" is preferable to "all inspired Scripture"; and (4) the term θεόπνευστος should be understood in the passive sense, meaning that all Scripture originates with God himself.[27] Thus, it appears that if the Bible retains any revelatory value at all, it must be allowed to convey the very words of God, and no epistemology—Kantian or otherwise—should eliminate God's communication by way of intelligible propositions. Reflecting on Carl F. H. Henry's robust defense of Scripture as propositional revelation, Peter Hicks states,

> Henry's central thesis is that *God reveals and God speaks*. There is no reason why we should limit God to one form of revelation (through either a person or a book, through either encounter or concept). God reveals and speaks in a number of ways, in his creation, in general revelation, and supremely in Christ, the incarnate Word. But, additionally and foundationally, he is able to formulate and communicate truth in an epistemic word, in which he articulates truth verbally through "intelligent disclosure"; and this, in sovereign grace, he has chosen to do.[28]

With the false dichotomy of Kantian thought sufficiently removed, there remains no substantive reason to view the words of the Bible as anything other than God's actual words—God's direct revelation.

---

26. Lloyd-Jones, *Authority*, 50.

27. Lea and Griffin, *1, 2 Timothy, Titus*, 235–36.

28. Hicks, *Evangelicals and Truth*, 89–90. See Henry, *God, Revelation, and Authority*, 3:429–87.

On the one hand, Adam thinks that those who preclude proposition from revelation do so because they feel that propositional revelation breeds mere mental assent and not true faith. This conjecture clearly underlies Avery Dulles's very negative assessment of the propositional model. For him, "faith in the sense of a firm assent to the revealed truths contained in the authoritative sources" has "inadequacy to experience."[29] He alleges,

> The propositions in the Bible . . . are held to be revelation, irrespective of whether they actually illuminate the believer's own situation. In this approach, little appeal is made to the evocative power of the biblical images and symbols; little motivation is given to seek signs of God's presence in one's own life and experience; little allowance is made for the kind of faith that probes and questions.[30]

Brooks prefigures Dulles when he scorns "mechanism" in preaching. By mechanism, Brooks means "the disposition of the preacher to forget that the Gospel of Christ is primarily addressed to individuals" and the "tendency to work for the means instead of for the end."[31] Adam, though, points out the paucity of thinking that the "statement of doctrine is a powerless exercise" by reiterating that "the word of God is living and active."[32] He cites Paul Helm's comment:

> It is a curious and historical fact that while the idea that the Bible is God's special propositional revelation has been charged with replacing God himself by propositions about God, an examination of the literature during periods when such a view was dominant suggests the exact reverse. In the first Chapter of the *Westminster Confession of Faith* (often said to be the product of what is regarded as theological decadence, "Reformed Scholasticism"), we are told that it "pleased the Lord, at sundry times, and in diverse manners, *to reveal himself.*" And in the *Westminster Shorter Catechism*, Question 86, "What is faith in Jesus Christ?" is answered as follows: "Faith in Jesus Christ is a saving grace, whereby we receive and rest upon him alone for salvation, as he is offered to us in the gospel." In the eyes of the Westminster Divines at least the words and propositions of the

---

29. Dulles, *Models of Revelation*, 45–46.

30. Ibid., 50–51.

31. Brooks, *Lectures*, 19, 22.

32. Adam, *Speaking God's Words*, 20.

gospel are not a barrier to faith in Christ, they are a necessary condition of that faith.[33]

In other words, biblical propositions do not concern only abstractions and impersonal facts. The Word of God rather calls its hearer to a personal faith in a personal Christ, and remains "sharper than any two-edged sword, and piercing as far as the division of soul and spirit, of both joints and marrow, and able to judge the thoughts and intentions of the heart" (Heb 4:12). Besides, as in any other relationship, receiving facts and information about a person is a natural, fitting, and necessary means for knowing that individual.

On the other hand, Adam discovers a more sinister motive behind the assault on propositional revelation—namely, that of sinful unbelief:

> Since the idea of God speaking is so fundamental to the Bible, why are we so reluctant to accept it? . . . People prefer a God who does not speak because he makes less clear demands, asks no questions, makes no promises, and threatens no punishments. One reason people prefer the company of dumb animals to that of humans is that dumb animals make fewer demands, ask no questions and make no promises. Nowadays this rejection of the meaning and purpose of God goes even deeper. The postmodern move against meaning in words, and against words themselves, is part of an attempt to create not only a world without God but a universe without meaning.[34]

Brooks certainly would have rejected the allegation that unbelief underlies his notion of truth and his preaching model. His sermons run replete with the idea that God speaks and makes known his will.[35] In fact, it should be noted that Brooks asserted his notions of truth and revelation to preserve Christian belief in the face of nineteenth-century intellectual challenges.[36] Nevertheless, it remains important to recognize that his disgust with regard to doctrinal formulations and concentration on personality distinctly fall in line with a larger trend that suppresses God's ability to speak in linguistic propositions.

33. Helm, *Divine Revelation*, 27.

34. Adam, *Speaking God's Words*, 23–24.

35. For example, see Brooks, "Living Epistles," 111.

36. Harp, *Brahmin Prophet*, 5.

The Necessity of Propositional Revelation for Preaching

Propositional revelation is a great and necessary preaching foundation. The belief that God has revealed himself in intelligible human language forms "the fulcrum of the Christian faith and of Christian preaching."[37] Indeed, "without God's Words there can be no ministry of the Word. If God is dumb, we may speak, but we cannot speak God's words, for there are none to speak."[38] Stott proclaims,

> Scripture affirms that God has spoken both through historical deeds and through explanatory words, and that the two belong indissolubly together. Even the Word made flesh, the climax of God's progressive self-revelation, would have remained enigmatic if it were not that he also spoke and that his apostles both described and interpreted him.
>
>   Here then is a fundamental conviction about the living, redeeming, and self-revealing God. It is the foundation on which all Christian preaching rests. We should never presume to occupy a pulpit unless we believe in this God. . . . If we are not sure of this, it would be better to keep our mouth shut.[39]

Even Herbert H. Farmer—who embraced a Barthian, neoorthodox approach to Scripture—nonetheless acknowledged that, even when revelation is conceived as an event, it must remain communicable. In his book, *The Servant of the Word,* he explains,

> Christianity is a religion of revelation; its central message is a declaration, proclamation that God has met the darkness of the human spirit with a great unveiling of succoring light and truth. The revelation moreover is historical, that is to say, it is given primarily through events which in the first place can only be reported and affirmed. As we have already said, no merely internal reflection can arrive at historical events. If a man is to be saved, he must be confronted again and again with the givenness of Christ.[40]

Albert Mohler points out how Farmer tacitly "argued that the unique authority of Christian preaching comes from the authority of revelation and, in particular, the Bible. Against those who maintained that revela-

---

37. Mohler, "A Theology of Preaching," 14.

38. Adam, *Speaking God's Words*, 25.

39. Stott, *Between Two Worlds*, 95–96.

40. Farmer, *Servant of the Word*, 86.

tion was basically internal, emotional, and relational, Farmer argued that it was given."[41]

Brooks's Fallacy: Internal Revelation and Homiletical Speculation

Long before the influence of romanticism or the rise of neoorthodoxy, Martin Luther loathed the faults of internal revelation. Wary of the dangers of spiritualism, he constantly stressed the nature of the gospel as a *verbum externum*—an external word—and despised those who "set themselves up as shrewd judges between the spirit and the letter."[42] He commented, "We all know from experience that our mind and thoughts are so uncertain, slippery and unstable, that if we want to ask a serious question or think about God without words and Scripture, we will be a hundred miles away from our first thoughts before we even know it." For him, the notion of internal revelation "is the source, power, and might of all the heresies," and "everything that boasts of being from the Spirit apart from such a word . . . is of the devil."[43]

If a theory of internal revelation produces dubious and precarious spirituality, then so does any homiletical model based upon it. Predictably, a survey of Brooks's sermons reveals just a scant presence of a biblical word, but a repository of romantic notions and methods. Gillis Harp observes:

> Brooks's popular published sermons illustrate this characteristic fondness for the aesthetic, the symbolic, and the sentimental. Tone and mood often became more important than doctrinal content; an appealing metaphor with literary resonance might be more sought after than sticking close to the original meaning of a particular text. . . . Argument by analogy rather than by logical reasoning was common.[44]

Indeed, Brooks typically—in Robert Dabney's terminology—employed "a fragment of the Word as a mere motto"[45] and leaped analogously into a discussion of one of his anthropological themes without any contextual analysis or serious exegesis. For instance, his sermon titled "The

41. Mohler, "Primacy of Preaching," 3.
42. Luther, quoted in Bayer, *Theology the Lutheran Way*, 51.
43. Ibid., 55, 51.
44. Harp, *Brahmin Prophet*, 214.
45. Dabney, *Sacred Rhetoric*, 75.

Candle of the Lord" (discussed briefly in chapter 3) takes the phrase, "The spirit of man is the lamp of the Lord," from Proverbs 20:27 and proceeds to assert the affinity between the divine and human natures. By completely ignoring the latter half of the verse, Brooks turns the proverb upside down and totally misses its point. When the second phrase, "searching all the innermost parts of his being," is considered with the initial phrase, it becomes clear that the proverb teaches that the Lord is the candle surveying the heart of a man. Brooks enacts the same ploy in a sermon titled "The Giant with the Wounded Heel," when he presents the woman's offspring in Genesis 3:15 as a metaphor for universal humanity, instead of a *protoevangelion* of Christ.[46] Along with others who dismiss the propositional nature of revelation, Brooks did not preach without propositions, but simply preached different propositions from those presented in the Bible.[47]

Brooks's fallacious biblical interpretations originate from his commitment to an internal notion of revelation. For him, preaching based on external authority "loses the clear conviction of the present Christ," but his careless use of Scripture and ambivalence regarding key Christian doctrines provide no clear conviction about Jesus at all, save perhaps Christ's desire that humans follow the Lord's will. In the *Lectures*, Brooks asserts, "On one thing only we may speak with authority, and that is the will of God." He fails to explain, though, how one comes to know the Lord's will apart from God's externally revealed words. Brooks would likely affirm that people should simply look to the person of Christ, and his heightened anthropology—without the separation caused by original sin—certainly allows for reliable revelation through instinct and introspection. However, evangelical theology dictates and Brooks's preaching demonstrates that, without Scripture's authoritative words, "The remembered Christ becomes the imagined Christ, shaped by the religiosity and the unconscious desires of his worshipers."[48]

In Brooks's essay called "The New Theism," he contends that, just as one bids a child to open his or her hand to get a better grip, Christians

---

46. Brooks, "Giant with the Wounded Heel," 95.

47. Craddock attempts to convey a method for preaching a didactic text within his revelatory framework. He presents one of his sermons, based on 1 Cor 8:1–13, as a case study but, in the end, he completely misses the point of the passage. Craddock, "Occasion-Text-Sermon," 59–71.

48. Smart, *Strange Silence*, 7.

should loosen their hold on the traditional concept of doctrine. He describes such loosening as "preparatory to a better tightening."[49] Harp lucidly interrogates the claim:

> If both the biblical and dogmatic bases of Christianity are substantially redefined, then what non-negotiable core is the community hand of faith going to fix its grip more tightly upon? Brooks would have probably replied that the Incarnation constituted the essential core here, but if this dogma is rooted in an essentially subjective argument, without an infallible bible [*sic*] and/or an authoritative confessional standard, could the center hold?[50]

More recently, when Stanley Grenz similarly attempted to "renew the center" of evangelicalism by reconstructing theology without propositional revelation, Albert Mohler replied by calling it a "center without a circumference," meaning that it could not sustain or enforce any doctrinal boundaries whatsoever.[51] Brooks's preaching model suffers the same deficiency. Preaching disconnected from proposition quickly is reduced to human speculation—a dumbing down made evident by the way that Brooks filled biblical jargon with romantic ideology. With respect to conveying Christian convictions, he gave preaching a dismal standard of success, confessing, "In much of what one preaches he is satisfied if men take home what he says as the utterance of one who has thought upon the subject and wishes them to think and judge."[52] Contrasted to Paul's exhortation for Timothy to "preach the word" and to "speak these things and exhort and reprove with all authority" (2 Tim 4:2; Titus 2:15), Brooks's thoughts about preaching seem a far cry from what the apostle intended. For one who was named the "prince of preachers,"[53] Brooks advanced a strange homiletical nobility—namely, one without any authority. Craddock certainly agreed with him, but evangelical preachers must not do so. In Brooks's scheme, "truth through personality" is perilously short on truth.

---

49. Brooks, "New Theism," 160.

50. Harp, *Brahmin Prophet*, 174.

51. Mohler, "Reformist Evangelicalism," 131–51. See Grenz, *Theology for the Community of God*; idem, *Renewing the Center*.

52. Brooks, *Lectures*, 86.

53. Perry, *Episcopate in America*, 330.

"TRUTH THROUGH PERSONALITY" AND THE OBSTACLE
OF INCARNATIONAL PREACHING

Brooks's appeal to Christ's incarnation as the center of his beliefs and ground of his preaching serves as a "thin coating of Evangelical theology"[54] over an anthropocentric notion of internal, individual revelation. As the phrase suggests, however, "truth through personality" exists more as a method of communication than as a statement about the nature of truth—emphasizing that, just as truth is revealed incarnationally, it is similarly transferred by means of human personality. Indeed, according to Alexander Allen, the conviction that "truth and moral efficiency in the will . . . pass from person to person through the medium of personality" constitutes the "leading idea" of Brooks's preaching concept.[55] Brooks freely asserted that his thoughts on the communicative aspect of preaching were grounded in Christ's incarnation, contending in his *Lectures on Preaching* that a preacher's only leadership "comes as the leadership of the Incarnation came," and that preaching is the "continuation" of the incarnation "out to the minutest ramifications."[56]

The Trend toward Incarnational Preaching Models

Since the time of Brooks's *Lectures*, the idea that preaching finds its basis in Christ's incarnation has become an increasingly pronounced theme in theological discussions of preaching. Michael J. Quicke aptly captures the trend when he writes, "God chooses to incarnate his Word in flesh and his words in a preacher's flesh."[57] McDill even offers a definition for an incarnational preaching model:

> The person of Christ, as fully God and fully man, serves as a model for all ministry. In preaching this model portrays the two elements of truth and personality. The very Word of God is proclaimed by a very human agent. This is God's method of making Himself known.[58]

---

54. Newton, *Yesterday with the Fathers*, 24.

55. Allen, *Life and Letters*, 2:305.

56. Brooks, *Lectures*, 85, 7.

57. Quicke, *360-Degree Preaching*, 93.

58. McDill, *Moment of Truth*, 25.

Homileticians across a wide swath of the theological spectrum speak uniformly of incarnational preaching, but without uniformity concerning what it means. Three general trends predominate. First of all, for some, such as David Brown, Greg Heisler, Stephen Olford, and Quicke, the call for incarnational preaching consists of an appeal for authenticity—the embodiment of biblical truth in the preacher's person. Heisler claims, "What people need to see in the pulpit is someone who has been changed and transformed by the truth he is proclaiming, not an imposter under the pretense of false spirituality. . . . As a preacher, you are an incarnate testimony of what your text is saying."[59] In this manner, incarnational preaching becomes a reminder that a pastor's life should be consistent with the message preached.

Second, other homileticians insist that an incarnational approach ensures the relevance of preaching to contemporary times. Clyde Fant, who contends that the incarnation "is the truest theological model for preaching," declares, "Jesus, who was the Christ, most perfectly said God to us because the eternal Word took on human flesh in a contemporary situation. Preaching cannot do otherwise."[60] McDill likewise argues forcefully that the "incarnational theme" creates "a continuing stress in preaching." According to him,

> On the one side is the "faith once delivered," the Word of God. On the other is the contemporary human situation, the particular context in which each sermon must be preached. Preaching, in this sense, is all human, and, at the same time, all divine. . . . The Bible in his hand is the divine Word of God. But he himself is part of this present age, a human messenger who clothes the word with his own personality in the sermon.[61]

Charles Cosgrove, W. Dow Edgerton, and Leonora Tisdale make similar missiological implications, attesting that Christ's incarnation furnishes a format for contextualizing the gospel within differing cultures.[62]

Third, still others utilize the incarnation in a manner that attributes a sacramental function to preaching. Dietrich Bonhoeffer notes,

59. Heisler, *Spirit-Led Preaching*, 98.

60. Fant, *Preaching for Today*, 70.

61. McDill, *Moment of Truth*, 25.

62. Cosgrove and Edgerton, *In Other Words*, 36–62; Tisdale, *Preaching as Local Theology*, 32–40.

> The proclaimed word has its origin in the incarnation of Jesus Christ. . . . The proclaimed word is the incarnate Christ himself. . . . Therefore the proclaimed word is not a medium of expression for something else, something which lies behind it, but rather it is Christ himself walking through his congregation as the word.[63]

William Willimon extends Bonhoeffer's thoughts by postulating an extremely close relationship between preaching and the incarnation:

> Everyone who speaks of this Incarnate One will find that his or her speaking participates in this same veiling and unveiling that characterized the Word Made Flesh.
>
> The Incarnation is the great mystery that makes preaching possible. . . . Preaching is a divinely wrought, miraculous act. Preaching is God's speech. Preaching is God's chosen means of self-revelation. If a sermon "works," it does so as a gracious gift of God, a miracle no less than the virginal conception of Jesus by the Holy Spirit. One reason why Christians tend to believe in the likelihood of miracles like the virgin birth of Jesus or the resurrection of Christ is that we have experienced miracles of similar order, if not similar magnitude, in our own lives as we have listened to a sermon. . . . Preaching is not only talk about God but miraculous talk by God.[64]

This strong application of the incarnation raises the persistent issue of whether or not the preaching of God's Word is God's Word, as the Second Helvetic Confession affirms.[65] While a sacramental notion of preaching found a voice during the Reformation,[66] the Second Helvetic Confession itself does not necessarily require it. In fact, the paragraph that follows the phrase, *praedicatio verbi Dei est verbum Dei* ("the preaching of the Word of God is the Word of God"), does not expound the idea, but rather conveys its implications—namely, that "when this Word of God is now preached in the church by preachers lawfully called, we believe that the very Word of God is preached, and received of the faithful."[67] Consequently, the confession aims to encourage hearers to receive the Word when preached more than it does to conjecture that preaching is itself the Word. Furthermore, Henry Bullinger, the author of the confes-

---

63. Bonhoeffer, *Worldly Preaching*, 129.

64. Willimon, *Proclamation and Theology*, 55–56.

65. Schaff, *Creeds of Christendom*, 3:237.

66. Meuser, "Luther as Preacher," 136.

67. Ibid.

sion, makes this same emphasis in his sermon series pertaining to the Word of God.[68] On the whole, it seems best to maintain that "preaching is *speaking God's words*," or that "preaching conveys the message of God when we preach and teach the words of Scripture."[69]

The Ontological Obstacle of Incarnational Preaching

Though rarely explored, significant problems arise when homileticians closely correlate the task of preaching and Christ's incarnation. The main problem concerns the ontological relationship between the preacher and the Word of God. As the incarnation itself was a "hypostatic union" between the divine and human natures[70]—the very Word in flesh (John 1:14)—any talk of preaching as an "incarnational" event must wrestle with the ontological inference made by the term. While the sacramental approach to incarnational preaching at least raises the issue, none of the correlative models attempts to delineate the nature of the relationship. Some points of likeness between preaching and Christ's incarnation certainly can be acknowledged—such as authenticity, embodiment, relevance, and contextualization—but simply identifying these similarities does not do enough to establish the incarnation as the theological ground for preaching.

Nowhere does the Bible state that preaching should be modeled after Christ's incarnation, nor do the terms used for preaching in the New Testament imply an incarnational union between the preacher and the Word. The term κηρύσσω, for example, meaning "to proclaim," appears more than fifty times in the New Testament. It usually is translated "preach," "preaching," or "preached" (Mark 1:38; Acts 19:13; 2 Cor 11:4; Gal 2:2).[71] Another significant term related to preaching is εὐαγγελίζω, meaning "to bring good news" (Rom 10:15; 1 Cor 9:16; Gal 1:16).[72] In some instances, the New Testament authors employ various terms for referring to acts of preaching, even if they do not utilize the specific word for preaching.[73] Such terms are διδάσκω, meaning "to impart di-

---

68. Bullinger, *Decades*, 69–80.

69. York and Decker, *Preaching with Bold Assurance*, 22; Adam, *Speaking God's Words*, 120.

70. Grudem, *Systematic Theology*, 558.

71. BDAG 431.

72. Ibid., 317.

73. Brown et al., *Steps to the Sermon*, 5.

vine truth through teaching" (1 Cor 4:17); διαλέγομαι, which means "to reason with others with a view to persuasion" (Acts 17:2); λαλεῖν, which means "to talk or discourse" (Acts 4:20); and παρακαλεῖν, which means "to admonish" (Titus 1:9).[74] While each of these terms recognizes and even requires the agency of human personality, none associates the preacher's personality with God's Word in an incarnational manner.

Building on Paul Ricoeur's remarks regarding Isaiah 43:8–13, Thomas Long holds that the role of "witness" is the most consistent biblical preaching image because it includes the observation and declaration of facts as well as personal conviction, experience, and loyalty.[75] Indeed, in the Gospel of John, as soon as the author makes the striking declaration that the "Word was with God, and the Word was God" (John 1:1), he immediately interjects, "There came a man sent from God, whose name was John. He came as a witness, to testify about the Light" (John 1:6–7). Later—in the same chapter—after John asserts the profound thought that "the Word became flesh," he again quickly purports that "John testified about Him" (John 1:14–15). John deliberately contrasts the incarnate Word to the one who bears witness to that Word.[76] Barth recognizes the difference and avows that John the Baptist, not Jesus, is the "prototype . . . of all attestation, in the biblical sense. And John says everything that can be said about himself in distinction from and in relation to Christ."[77] Indeed, Jesus himself commissioned the disciples as "witnesses" (Luke 24:48; Acts 1:8), and Paul's apostolic preaching embraces this same role. Paul consistently positions himself throughout the New Testament as a personal witness to a received message—not as a replica of the incarnation:

> But I do not consider my life of any account as dear to myself, so that I may finish my course and the ministry which I received from the Lord Jesus, to testify solemnly of the gospel of the grace of God (Acts 20:24).
>
> For I delivered to you as of first importance what I also received, that Christ died for our sins according to the Scriptures, and that

74. BDAG 192, 185, 463, 617.

75. Long, *Witness of Preaching*, 45–50.

76. Interestingly, Willimon makes this same point immediately prior to endorsing a sacramental form of incarnational preaching. Willimon, *Proclamation and Theology*, 50–51.

77. Barth, *CD* 1/2:231.

he was buried, and that he was raised on the third day according to the Scriptures, and that he appeared to Cephas, then to the twelve (1 Cor 15:3).

For I would have you know, brethren, that the gospel which was preached by me is not according to man. For I neither received it from man, nor was I taught it, but I received it through a revelation of Jesus Christ (Gal 1:11–12).

One of Paul's statements might be understood to imply an incarnational motif, but a closer examination reveals no inconsistency with his position as a witness. Galatians 1:15–16 reads, "But when God . . . was pleased to reveal his Son in me so that I might preach him among Gentiles. . . ." Some comprehend this expression to infer a subjective revelation within the apostle,[78] but Ronald Fung lucidly shows that, while the phrase ἐν ἐμοὶ ("in me") stresses the intensely personal character of God's revelation to Paul, it nonetheless does not suggest an inward revelation without an external object. According to Fung, with "little doubt," the preceding phrase—"to reveal his Son"—refers to "Paul's vision of the risen Christ" on the Damascus road.[79] In fact, because of the following purpose clause, "so that I might preach," Timothy George interprets ἐν ἐμοὶ to mean something closer to "through me." The English Standard Version goes so far as to render the phrase as "to me." In sum, the task issued to, and carried out by, the apostles carries no incarnational thrust—no notion that the revelation of Christ arises from within a human personality. Instead, the New Testament perspective on preaching—consistent with a scriptural and propositional concept of revelation—fosters a model in which the message comes from God (externally) to the preacher, and then goes through the preacher to the hearers. The preacher exists as a personal witness to a divine message, not as a new incarnation of that message.

Christ's incarnation does, though, possess some preaching implications. On the practical level, the incarnation legitimately illustrates some of the aforementioned functional realities of preaching, such as authenticity, embodiment, relevance, and contextualization. The incarnation can serve as a perfect example of these dynamics, as long as they are not construed to turn the incarnation into the ontological model for preaching. On the theological level, the implications of the incarnation

78. See discussion in George, *Galatians*, 119–20.
79. Fung, *Epistle to the Galatians*, 64.

for preaching must be limited to an affirmation that God speaks, that he speaks through human agency, and that he has spoken supremely in the person of Jesus Christ. The miraculous incarnation permits preachers "to speak of God in the terms He has set for Himself—in the identity of Jesus the Christ."[80] For this reason, the incarnation is the truth to which preachers bear witness—not what they become.

Brooks's Deficiency: The Preacher Becomes the Word

Although they seem largely unaware of the problem, homileticians who hold preaching to incarnational standards propose both an impossibility and absurdity. The incarnation certainly was—and is—a demonstration of "truth through personality," yet it remains a supreme, *sui generis* event that human preachers cannot duplicate. The hypostatic union of the divine and human natures exists exclusively in the person of Jesus Christ. Stating—as Brooks did—that preaching is an extension of Christ's incarnation presents an association between the preacher's personality and the Word of God that causes heretical consequences. Undoubtedly, Brooks's heightened anthropology allows for an exceptionally close relation between the preacher and the Word, and facilitates a direct correlation between the incarnation and preaching. Indeed, his view that humans are incarnations-in-miniature—devoid of the stain of original sin and irrevocably children of God—makes Christ's incarnation the ground of all life and not just of preaching. Brooks emphasized the incarnation so freely—and linked his preaching with it so much—that some of his auditors began literally to consider him as another divine incarnation. A Boston workingman's letter to Brooks reads, "To me you reveal God as no other man does. . . . I can't think of you for ten consecutive minutes without forgetting all about you and thinking of God instead; and when I think of God and wonder how he will seem to me, it always comes round to trying to conceive of you enlarged infinitely in every way."[81] Applying such terminology to any person but Jesus borders on blasphemy (John 14:9) and reveals a fundamental error of Brooks's incarnational preaching concept—it too closely connects the preacher with God's Word.

John A. Huffman rightly contends that a preacher should always preserve a distinction between his person and the Word: "We dare not

---

80. Mohler, "Why Do We Preach?" lines 16–17.
81. Allen, *Life and Letters*, 3:460.

identify truth so closely with our own selfhood that we relativize it in our preaching to the point that the Word of God preached is a human word cut free from the written Word."[82] Evangelicals, affirming the realities of the separation caused by sin (Ps 51:5; Isa 59:2; Rom 5:12–14; Eph 2:3) and the impassable distinction between the Creator and the creature, must reject—theologically and ontologically—preaching models that correlate directly with Christ's incarnation. The preacher's ontological relationship with the Word is that of Paul, not Jesus. Preaching ought thus to be conceived more as a continuation of the apostolic model and not of the incarnation.

RHETORICAL *ĒTHOS*, THE GOSPEL, AND A PROBLEM FOR "TRUTH THROUGH PERSONALITY"

Beyond the theological and ontological difficulty raised by an incarnational notion of preaching, the persuasive method proposed by Brooks's "truth through personality" definition presents a rhetorical problem as well. His penchant for connecting every facet of preaching to Christ's incarnation results in a particularly heavy focus—not only on the preacher's personality, but additionally on the preacher's personal character. For him, the "making of a man" serves as the initial principle of preaching precisely because the embodiment of truth facilitates the transmission of character from one person to another.[83] Brooks remarks, "Nothing but fire kindles fire,"[84] by which he means that personal character in the preacher comprises the means of character formation in the hearers. Throughout his *Lectures*, Brooks insists upon the persuasive power of personal character. In the second lecture, "The Preacher Himself," he frankly states,

> And first among the elements of power which make success I must put the supreme importance of character, of personal uprightness and purity impressing themselves upon the men who witness them. . . . The truth must conquer, but it must first embody itself in goodness. . . . Whatever strange and scandalous eccentricities the ministry has sometimes witnessed, this is certainly true, and is always encouraging, that no man permanently succeeds in it who cannot make men believe that he is pure and

82. Huffman, "Role of Preaching in Ministry," 38.

83. Brooks, *Lectures*, 9, 43–45.

84. Ibid., 38.

> devoted, and the only sure and lasting way to make men believe
> in one's devotion and purity is to be what one wishes to be be-
> lieved to be.[85]

Brooks's thoughts on the role of character display remarkable consistency with the classical concept of rhetorical *ēthos*.[86] Aristotle included *ēthos*, along with *logos* and *pathos*, among the three artistic proofs available in the speaker's arsenal. He did not, however, place all three on equal footing. According to his *Rhetoric*, "We might almost affirm that . . . character is the most potent of all the means to persuasion."[87]

Classical Rhetoric and Contemporary Homiletics

Since Augustine's time, many Christian homileticians have followed Aristotle in elevating the power of rhetorical *ēthos*. In fact, Augustine, in *On Christian Doctrine*—the first Christian textbook on homiletical structure and procedure—nearly quotes Aristotle when he explains that "the life of the speaker has greater weight in determining whether he is obediently heard than any grandness of eloquence."[88] Later homileticians concur. John A. Broadus suggests that "the prime requisite to efficiency in preaching is earnest piety. . . . Much false theory and bad practice in preaching is connected with a failure to apprehend the fundamental importance of piety in the preacher."[89] Similarly, Bryan Chapell goes on to say, "The character and compassion of the minister more determine the quality of the message heard than the characteristics of the message preached."[90] As a general rule, homileticians highlight the importance of character, whether or not they engage in a sustained discussion of rhetorical *ēthos*.[91]

---

85. Ibid., 49–51.

86. *Ēthos* is spelled with the diacritical marking to denote the term as a Greek trans-literation and to distinguish it from the common English word "ethos," which means "custom" or "standard." See Resner, *Preacher and Cross*, 2.

87. Aristotle, *Rhetoric*, 8–9.

88. Augustine *On Christian Doctrine* 4.27.59.

89. Broadus, *Treatise*, 7–8.

90. Chapell, *Christ-Centered Preaching*, 30.

91. See Quicke, *360-Degree Preaching*, 93–95; McDill, *Moment of Truth*, 29–36; Olford, *Anointed Expository Preaching*, 43–47; Vines and Shaddix, *Power in the Pulpit*, 71–74.

Although homileticians share some common ground with Aristotle pertaining to the persuasive power of *ēthos*, there is no consensus regarding its nature and appropriate usage. Roughly, the term *ēthos* means "character," but the classical writers did not employ it in a technical sense.[92] Rather, each filled the concept with his own meaning, resulting in multiple and interrelated viewpoints. Chronologically, the major classical discussions of *ēthos* start with the Sophists and proceed to Plato, Aristotle, Cicero, and Quintilian.[93] Each discussion, though, turns on the issue of whether *ēthos* rests solely in the auditors' perception of the speaker's character, or if it exists in the speaker's actual character. In this regard, the classical writers may be placed along a continuum illustrated by Figure 1.

Emphasis on Perceived Character　　　　　　*Emphasis on Real Character*

Sophists　　　　Aristotle　　　　Cicero　　　　Quintilian　　　　Plato

Brooks maintains the importance of perceived character, but holds that possessing genuine character is the "sure and lasting way" to create the perception. In this manner, his approach aligns closely with that of Quintilian (AD 35–95), who notably claimed, "For if rhetoric is the science of speaking well, its end and highest aim is to speak well."[94] One detects a hint of the more pragmatic tendencies of the Sophists and Aristotle in Quintilian's thought. According to his *Institutio Oratoria*,

> For it is most important that he should himself possess or be thought to possess those virtues for the possession of which it is his duty, if possible, to commend his client as well, while the excellence of his own character will make his pleading all the more convincing and will be of the utmost service to the cases which he undertakes. For the orator who gives the impression of being a bad man while he is speaking, is actually speaking badly, since his words seem to be insincere owing to the absence of *ēthos* which would otherwise have revealed itself.[95]

Even his pragmatic concerns, however, preserve a very strong ethical component and a key emphasis on real character. Any division between

92. Anderson, *Glossary*, 61–62.

93. For a chronological discussion of the development of classical rhetoric, see Kennedy, *Classical Rhetoric*, 1–126.

94. Quintilian *Institutio Oratoria* 2.15.38.

95. Ibid., 6.2.17–18.

moral philosophy and rhetoric is unthinkable for him. He purports, "I should give my vote for virtuous living in preference to even supreme excellence in speaking. But in my opinion the two are inseparable. I hold that no one can be a true orator unless he is also a good man and, even if he could be, I would not have it so."[96] As a result, Quintilian defines rhetorical *ēthos* not merely as a tool for persuasion, but instead as "a good man, skilled in speaking."[97] With striking resemblance, Brooks acknowledges in his *Lectures*,

> It is not only necessary for a sermon that there should be a human being to speak to other human beings, but for a good sermon there must be a man who can speak well, whose nature stands in right relations to those to whom he speaks, who has brought his life close to theirs with sympathy. . . . The duty of making yourself acceptable to people, and winning by all manly ways their confidence in you, and in the truth which you tell, is one that is involved in the very fact of your being a preacher. . . . Here stands a man, and two other men are watching him. Both of them are studying his character.[98]

A classical approach to rhetorical *ēthos* works well in Brooks's character-focused homiletic, in which a heightened anthropology lets a preacher present himself as a genuinely good person. Evangelicals, though, must wrestle more deeply with the issue of rhetorical *ēthos* because they preach a message that implicates the preacher as a sinner. The apostle Paul, whose perspective on the matter is infinitely more binding than that of the classical writers, did not hesitate to make an appeal to *ēthos* (1 Thess 2:5–12), but also referred to himself as "foremost" among "sinners" (1 Tim 1:15). Understanding how Paul could affirm his *ēthos* on the one hand and openly confess his weakness on the other hand necessitates a deeper look into his relationship with rhetoric, in general, and his approach to *ēthos,* in particular.

Contemporary Perspectives on Paul's Approach to Rhetoric and Use of Ēthos

While most scholars agree that Paul's letters demonstrate his cognizance of classical rhetoric, there is no such consensus concerning Paul's rela-

96. Ibid., 1.2.3.
97. Ibid., 12.1.1.
98. Brooks, *Lectures*, 74–75.

tionship to it or utilization of it.[99] Some, such as George Kennedy, believe that Paul dismisses rhetoric altogether and flees from its use.[100] Others, such as Mario DiCicco, suggest that classical rhetoric so dominates Paul's culture and education that he employs it indiscriminately and perhaps even unknowingly.[101] The first view fails to recognize that Paul objected to rhetoric in rhetorically sophisticated ways.[102] The second viewpoint fails to identify the supernatural dynamic at work in Paul's preaching. Therefore, a reasonable perspective acknowledges the obvious presence of rhetorical elements within his discourse, but does not assume that his work is merely the skill of a clever rhetorician.[103] In the Corinthian correspondence, Paul admits to being persuasive (1 Cor 4:14), but rejects any notion that he is simply a good speaker.

> For Christ did not send me to baptize, but to preach the gospel, not in cleverness of speech, so that the cross of Christ would not be made void (1 Cor 1:17). . . . And when I came to you, brethren, I did not come with superiority of speech or of wisdom, proclaiming to you the testimony of God (1 Cor 2:1). . . . [M]y message and my preaching were not in persuasive words of wisdom (1 Cor 2:4).

Paul rather describes his preaching as a "demonstration of the Spirit and of power" (1 Cor 2:4) as he speaks in words not "taught by human wisdom, but in those taught by the Spirit" (1 Cor 2:13). Paul's reliance on

99. Christian preaching always sustains an awkward relationship with rhetoric. Early Latin fathers—such as Tertullian and Jerome—largely dismissed rhetoric as worldly, although they objected in a rhetorically sophisticated manner. Some of the Greek fathers—such as Justin Martyr, Clement of Alexandria, and Origen—were more accommodating. Augustine believed rhetoric to be a neutral tool that can be used for the gospel. See Resner, *Preacher and Cross*, 40–82; Hogan and Reid, *Connecting with the Congregation*, 12–13.

100. Kennedy nonetheless admits that certain elements of classical rhetoric appear in Paul. Kennedy, *Classical Rhetoric*, 131–32, 149.

101. DiCicco contends that Paul's claims to be "unskilled in speech" (2 Cor 11:6) should be taken in an ironic sense and not at face value. Furthermore, DiCicco claims that Paul's denial of rhetorical skill is only a disavowal of an "overtly ornamental and artificial style," and not a renunciation of his general persuasive abilities. DiCicco, *Paul's Use*, 23–28.

102. Resner, *Preacher and Cross*, 95.

103. Most scholars recognize the presence of rhetorical structures within Paul. See Kennedy, *Classical Rhetoric*, 149; Long, *Ancient Rhetoric*, 117–241. Mitchell convincingly demonstrates that 1 Corinthians reflects all the typical genre markers of classical deliberative rhetoric. Mitchell, *Paul and the Rhetoric of Reconciliation*, 24–61.

the Spirit's persuasive power does not mean, however, that he dismissed rhetoric altogether or that he implemented it indiscriminately. Instead, Paul prudently used rhetoric in ways that are "consistent with, even demanded by, the gospel and the kind of community that the gospel forms."[104] Paul's rhetoric is one transformed by his message and empowered by the Spirit.

Inadequate opinions of Paul's use of *ēthos* are derived from the truncated views of his rhetorical stance. Those who want to mitigate the presence of rhetoric in Paul, like Gerhard Friedrich and Duane Litfin, focus on the preacher's role as "herald" (κῆρυξ, κηρύσσω) to an extent that downplays the person of the preacher and the convincing force of *ēthos*. According to Friedrich, New Testament preachers are "heralds—no more. It is not their moral blamelessness nor their Christianity which decides the worth or efficacy of their preaching."[105] Likewise, Litfin writes,

> The principles of rhetorical adaptation are irrelevant to the κῆρυξ. . . . That sort of thing belongs to the persuader. The herald's task is not to create a persuasive message at all, but to convey effectively the already articulated message of another. The matter of rendering that message persuasive is not his affair.[106]

The "herald" view, with regard to Paul's preaching, is correct in so far that it maintains a boundary between the preacher and the Word; it is accurate in that no human rhetorical device can render the gospel effective. Friedrich and Litfin, however, take the "herald" concept too far, running the risk of subverting the person and *ēthos* of the preacher altogether. Paul—while faithfully heralding the gospel—nevertheless stressed that "stewards of the mysteries of God" must be found "trustworthy," and recognized that the Lord will "disclose the motives of men's hearts" (1 Cor 4:2, 5). He exhorted Timothy to "prescribe and teach" and to commit himself to "exhortation," but urged Timothy to be "an example of those who believe" and to "pay close attention" to himself as well (1 Tim 4:11–16). For Paul, faithful gospel proclamation places great demands on the preacher's *ēthos*.

In contrast to Friedrich and Litfin, DiCicco thinks that Paul utilized classical *ēthos* proofs wholesale and unaltered. According to DiCicco,

104. Resner, *Preacher and Cross*, 83.

105. *TDNT* 710.

106. Litfin, *St. Paul's Theology*, 196.

Paul secured for himself the audience's goodwill by drawing directly upon the dimensions of *ēthos* discussed by "Aristotle, Cicero, and the other rhetorical theorists."[107] Walking through 2 Corinthians 10–13, DiCicco contends that Paul builds an *ēthos* argument in the passage from the "four quarters" of classical *ēthos* persuasion: "from his own person, from the persons of his opponents, from the persons of his audience, and from the case itself."[108] DiCicco continues,

> From his own person, Paul captures the goodwill of the Corinthians by boasting of his own acts and services without arrogance. . . . From the person of his opponents, Paul brings the Corinthians to his viewpoint by presenting a very negative picture of his detractors as arrogant in their claims, self-seeking in their motives, and intolerable in their use of advantages. He gains his auditors' respect and attention by showing them what honorable esteem he has for them, how perceptive he believes they are in detecting frauds, and how eagerly he awaits their sensible judgment in a matter of great importance. Finally, from the case at hand, Paul gets an intelligent hearing by arguing from his interpretation of the Gospel as the authentic teaching about Christ and by disparaging the gospel of his opponents as full of "sophistries and proud pretension" (10:5). Throughout . . . Paul weaves together these four types of argument to project an ἦθος of trustworthiness, competence, and concern which operates as a powerful rhetorical proof for the genuineness of his message.[109]

DiCicco's evaluation contains some truth, but overlooks the radical impact of the gospel on Paul's rhetorical *ēthos*. Because Paul's gospel reveals the depravity of human nature and the need for rebirth, Paul could not present himself as a good man by his own merits. The Pauline passages in which DiCicco detects classical rhetorical *ēthos* actually possess strong evidence that Paul used *ēthos* in a fundamentally different way. In 2 Corinthians, even as Paul senses the necessity for defending his ministry, he calls his personal commendation "foolishness" and "according to the flesh" (2 Cor 11:1, 17, 21). Instead of reveling in his accomplishments, he boasts in his "weaknesses, so that the power of Christ may dwell" in him (2 Cor 12:9). Moreover, Paul speaks about a "thorn in the flesh," which prevents any self-exaltation (2 Cor 12:7), and ultimately maintains that

107. DiCicco, *Paul's Use*, 78–79.

108. Ibid., 78.

109. Ibid., 79.

God is the One who commends his ministry. "For it is not he who commends himself that is approved," Paul writes, "but he whom the Lord commends" (2 Cor 10:18). Paul indeed employed rhetorical *ēthos*, but in a wholly different sense than did the classics.

Paul's "Reverse-Ēthos" as a Rhetorical Model

Among the scholarly perspectives pertaining to Paul's rhetorical *ēthos*, the work of André Resner Jr. most consistently applies Paul's general rhetorical approach to his particular use of *ēthos*. Throughout the Pauline corpus, and especially in 1 Corinthians 1–4, Resner identifies a rhetorical trend, which he calls "reverse-*ēthos*." He argues that Paul employs *ēthos* in a way that turns the concept upside down with a "countervailing Christian perspective."[110] For Paul, there are only two ways of knowing. The first way is knowledge "according to the flesh" (1 Cor 1:26; 2 Cor 1:17; 5:16; 10:2–3; 11:18), which places a premium on externals like image, accomplishments, and human ability. Paul knows that his audience typically considers "things as they are outwardly" (2 Cor 10:7) and judges the *ēthos* of a speaker "according to the flesh," making both him and his message appear as "foolishness" (1 Cor 1:18–25). Paul's alternative, though, is "a way of knowing that is shaped by the new framework for discernment grounded in, and proceeding from, the cross-event-proclaimed."[111] According to Resner, Paul asserts this cross-centered epistemology: "And when I came to you, brethren, I did not come with superiority of speech or wisdom, proclaiming to you the testimony of God. For I determined to know nothing among you except Jesus Christ, and Him crucified" (1 Cor 2:1–2).[112] Paul—when he visited the Corinthians—obviously addressed many issues beyond the simple fact of Jesus' crucifixion, but nonetheless the cross forms the epistemological lens through which he viewed all reality. Thus, any discussion of *ēthos* falls under the rubric of the *logos* of the cross. Resner explains, "For Paul, true *ēthos* is derivative not of social and cultural expectations but of an expectation that arises from the nature of the gospel."[113]

---

110. Resner, *Preacher and Cross*, 105–6.

111. Ibid., 109.

112. Ibid., 112.

113. Ibid., 130.

On the whole, the Pauline corpus attributes persuasion to the Spirit's power, but still concentrates on *ēthos* as a necessary corollary of the gospel. For Paul, *ēthos* does not so much lend credibility to *logos*, but rather *logos* dominates and guides *ēthos*. Paul's *logos* indeed becomes the "epistemic guide for all matters in the rhetorical situation of Christian proclamation," including *ēthos*.[114] Consequently, in Paul's thought, the proof lies ultimately with the *ēthos* of God and not with the *ēthos* of the preacher. Resner explains,

> Before Paul moves on to his first appeal (*parakaleō* in the *propositio* of 1:10), he prefaces his personal *ēthos* argument with a divine *ēthos* assertion: "God is faithful; by him you were called into the fellowship of his Son, Jesus Christ our Lord" (1:9). It is not the human preacher's *ēthos* which makes efficacious the gospel. Rather, it is God's trustworthiness. A better question than the one which was common in classical rhetorical situations ("Can this human orator be trusted?") is the question which the cross-event-proclaimed necessitates: "Can this God be trusted?" Thus, preacher *ēthos* ironically consists in the preacher not being morally pure or credible by means of his or her own accomplishments, since this is in fact in conflict with the message of Jesus Christ crucified. The preacher must be a sinner in need, not "saint," if by this is meant living above the mire of the human predicament. This means that far from being morally pure ("good"), or culturally credible in such a way as to predispose the hearer to accepting the message (antecedent *ēthos*), part of the preacher's role includes having an ongoing cognizance and humility to acknowledge his or her own complicity in sin—sin for which Christ's sacrifice alone was efficacious. Refocusing his audience from himself as preacher to God as guarantor allows the theology of the cross (1 Cor 1:18–25) to inform the way in which the *ēthos* of the preacher in the Christian rhetorical situation is to be differentiated from the classical rhetorical perspective.[115]

Because the *logos* of the cross has independent credibility from God, Paul admits that the true gospel can be preached even by pretentious men (Phil 1:15–18). The gospel's God-attested nature does not imply, however, that the preacher's *ēthos* is unimportant. In fact, the *logos* of the cross implicates the preacher's *ēthos* by making claims on his life and demanding of him the same that it requires of all.

114. Ibid., 153.
115. Ibid., 107.

In Paul's thought, the preacher must build *ēthos*, but he must create it according to the cross by surrendering his character ultimately to God's scrutiny (1 Cor 4:3–5) and by embracing self-effacement as a rhetorical stance. In the Corinthian correspondence, one can easily detect Paul's hesitancy to describe his accomplishments (2 Cor 11:1, 16; 12:1–6), readiness to speak of his weaknesses (1 Cor 4:9–13; 2 Cor 11:30; 12:7–10), and constant effort to turn the attention away from himself to God's power and grace (2 Cor 2:17; 4:5–7; 12:19). Paul says, "For our proud confidence is this: the testimony of our conscience, that in holiness and godly sincerity, not in fleshly wisdom but in the grace of God, we have conducted ourselves in the world, and especially toward you" (2 Cor 1:12). Viewed "according to the flesh," such self-effacement destroys the rhetorical power of *ēthos*. In the scheme of the gospel, though, "This shifting and refocusing of emphasis away from self as preacher and to God as source of preaching's power acts to build the kind of preacher-*ēthos* which does attribute credibility to the preacher of the gospel."[116]

Brooks's Incompatibility: Classical Ēthos and the Christian Gospel

Brooks's classically aligned approach to *ēthos* stands in stark contrast to that of the apostle Paul. Brooks's message—his *logos*—is that the "awakening of the spiritual element in any man is just his coming to know and act on the knowledge that he is a child of God."[117] His anthropocentric "gospel" consists of "natural virtues held up to the light of Christ,"[118] and hence his preaching becomes an effort in developing the character that is inborn in every person. As a result, Brooks's homiletic employs a form of rhetorical *ēthos* very similar to that of the classical writers—namely, "good man, skilled in speaking." In his plan, the preacher who possesses character inwardly and displays it outwardly is well-positioned to foster the same in others. Paul's writings, however, proclaim a different message that requires a fundamentally dissimilar approach to rhetorical *ēthos*. Paul's gospel holds that "all have sinned and fall short of the glory of God, being justified as a gift by His grace through the redemption which is in Christ Jesus; whom God displayed publicly as a propitiation in His blood through faith" (Rom 3:23–25). The *logos* proclaimed in the

116. Ibid.
117. Brooks, "Spiritual Man," 300.
118. Brooks, "Light of the World," 8–9.

Pauline literature prevents a classical approach to *ēthos* and demands what Resner defines as reverse-*ēthos*—a rhetorical stance that is consistent with the gospel. For this reason, Brooks's mode of persuasion remains antithetical to the Christian gospel and fails as an evangelical preaching model.

CONCLUSION

"Truth through personality," as it stands in Brooks's *Lectures* and is displayed throughout his preaching, asserts internal revelation against the biblical affirmation that God speaks in intelligible propositions; suggests an incarnational idea of preaching that does not maintain the necessary distinction between the preacher and God's Word; and presents an overly character-driven model of persuasion that is fundamentally incompatible with the gospel. These faults rise directly from Brooks's heightened anthropology, which avows humanity's natural and unchangeable sonship to God; universalizes Christ's incarnation; eliminates the need for substitutionary atonement; and redefines conversion as self-discovery and building character.[119] Within this theological framework, Brooks could unpretentiously advance a homiletical model, which—due to humanity's natural affinity with God and existence as an extension of God's life[120]—permits truth to arise within the preacher, promotes the preacher's union with God's Word, and embraces the reality and power of personal character. In other words, Brooks reformulated the Christian gospel into an anthropocentric and humanistic message, giving birth to an equally anthropocentric and humanistic homiletic.

For the most part, it appears that evangelicals tend to cite—and even endorse—"truth through personality" without any real awareness of what Phillips Brooks intended by the idea. For example, Stott and Jerry Vines both quote his definition and proceed to profess stoutly evangelical convictions concerning the nature and function of preaching.[121] Some, such as Quicke, extract Brooks's phrase as a slogan and employ it as a springboard into their own thoughts on preaching.[122] McDill

119. Brooks, "Spiritual Man," 300; idem, *Influence of Jesus*, 12; idem, "Conqueror from Edom," 41–55; idem, "New Experiences," 300–301; idem, "Opening of the Eyes," 212.

120. Brooks, "Need of Enthusiasm," 297–99.

121. Stott, *Between Two Worlds,* 266–95; Vines and Shaddix, *Power in the Pulpit,* 25–26.

122. Quicke, *360-Degree Preaching,* 87–97.

goes even further, contending not only that the definition "rings true," but that Brooks's work "ranks with the finest books on homiletics."[123] Considering the evangelical convictions of these authors and the conservative nature of their work, it seems highly doubtful that they would treat Brooks so lavishly if they realized the revelatory, theological, and rhetorical notions present within "truth through personality." The tendency to allude to his famous definition probably comes from the very broadness of the phrase itself, which Adam notes is "general enough to include the stand-up comic or a good actor!"[124] This extensive generality, in typical Brooks fashion, allows a homiletician to fill it with individual ideology. Evangelicals should reconsider—and even refrain from—endorsing Brooks and his famous definition, however, to eliminate the risk of sanctioning a concept that purports quite serious deviations from evangelical Christianity. Perhaps evangelicals can gainfully employ the phrase, "truth through personality," but not by blindly citing Brooks and thereby tacitly sustaining his problematic concepts.

123. McDill, *Moment of Truth*, 23–24.
124. Adam, *Speaking God's Words*, 59.

5

"Truth through Personality": An Axiom Reconstructed

DESPITE THE HAZARDOUS DEFICIENCIES of Brooks's definition, the phrase "truth through personality" can be constructed in a manner consistent with evangelical Christianity—simply by supporting it with the one true Christian gospel. Behind and beneath "truth through personality," evangelicals must acknowledge the effects of Adam's sin on all humanity (Rom 5:12–14): namely, that "all have sinned and fall short of the glory of God" (Rom 3:23) and exist "by nature children of wrath" (Eph 2:3). The reality of sin and its consequences furnish a more accurate anthropology—one asserting that humanity is special, but desperately fallen. A biblical anthropology leads to, and facilitates, scriptural convictions concerning Christ's substitutionary atonement and the vital need for a new birth and not mere character development (2 Cor 5:21; 1 Pet 3:18; John 3:3–21; 2 Cor 5:17; Gal 6:15). From these primary evangelical doctrines emerges a formulation of "truth through personality" that appreciates the necessity for propositional revelation, recognizes the proper ontological distance between the preacher and God's Word, and embraces a gospel-driven persuasive model.

Even with these evangelical underpinnings, however, "truth through personality" serves the preaching task best when conceived as an axiom and not presented as a definition. A definition "establishes limits. It sets down what must be included and excluded by a term or statement."[1] Considering that Brooks's slogan has been utilized to support a plethora of preaching ideologies, providing definition is one feat that "truth through personality" fails to accomplish. Yet, the expression possesses some self-evident intrinsic merit—to which its vast popular-

---

1. Robinson, *Biblical Preaching*, 142.

ity attests—that demonstrates its axiomatic nature. As an axiom, "truth through personality" proposes one essential preaching feature, but does not claim to include all necessary preaching components. Even as an axiom, though, "truth through personality" must encompass evangelical convictions if it is to offer an evangelical vision for preaching. Therefore, this chapter reconstructs "truth through personality" as an evangelical preaching axiom that is filled with, and carries out, evangelical beliefs.

THE ANTHROPIC NATURE OF SPECIAL REVELATION AND GOD'S ACCOMMODATION IN PREACHING

First of all, reconstructing "truth through personality" in an evangelical manner requires an admission that God—in fact—has spoken his external, propositional revelation through the medium of human personality.[2] While, at times, God's speech came directly to humans, John Calvin's tenet for divine communication remains accurate to the core: "God does not speak openly from heaven but employs men as His instruments."[3] Truly, God's special revelation of himself and his saving message come as "mediated" revelation.[4] God's words of personal address (Exod 3:4–10; Matt 3:17); his speech through human lips (Deut 18:18–20; Jer 1:9); his words in written form (Exod 31:18; 2 Pet 1:20–21); and his words as the Word-in-flesh (John 1:14–18) all display God's condescension to human categories of thought and action.[5]

God employed human agency even when he revealed himself in Scripture. While some throughout church history have denied any human element in the event of inspiration and have opted for a perfunctory

---

2. "Personality" implies more than man's status as a created being because existing as a person "means to have a kind of independence—not absolute but relative." Such relative independence is derived from being made in God's image, which entails volitional ability, moral conscience, rationality, use of language, inner character, emotions, and behavior. "Personality" may be defined as a human being's "individual conscious existence . . . distinctly associated with his higher nature, the intellectual and moral." Hoekema, *Created in God's Image*, 5; Boyce, *Abstract of Systematic Theology*, 195.

3. Calvin, *Commentary on the Book of the Prophet Isaiah*, 3:172.

4. Erickson, *Christian Theology*, 204. "Special" revelation should be understood as God's supernatural communication of himself to particular individuals at definite times and places, as distinct from "general" revelation, which is God's revelation to all humanity at all times through the created order. Ibid., 177–223; Warfield, *Inspiration and Authority*, 74; Grudem, *Systematic Theology*, 47–50.

5. Erickson, *Christian Theology*, 213.

"dictation" theory, Carl F. H. Henry counters, "The writers of Scripture are not unhistorical phantoms whom the divine Spirit controls like mechanical robots. . . . Their various differences of personality and style carry over into the sacred literature."[6] The Bible's most explicit reference to its human authors indeed contends that "men moved by the Holy Spirit spoke from God" (1 Pet 1:20–21). Although this passage has been the source of some controversy, it clearly encourages the notion that "revelation was not a matter of passive reception. . . . God's inspiration did not mean a supersession of the normal mental functionings of the human authors."[7] Douglas Moo reiterates, "To deny the human element in Scripture is to ignore the reality of the individual personalities, writing styles, situations, etc., that make up much of the richness of God's Word."[8] When reading the Bible, one certainly cannot help but "sense the burning sarcasm of Isaiah; the tender, earnest pathos of Jeremiah; the philosophical leanings of John; the sharp, crisp logic of Paul."[9]

While the Bible is the infallible, inerrant Word of God, the words of Scripture remain inseparably as words written by human authors. Robert Stein succinctly states, "Christians, of course, believe that behind those books of the Bible stands the living God," but also, "No book of the Bible claims God as its immediate author."[10] This concept finds common expression in evangelical definitions of verbal-plenary inspiration. Article VIII of "The Chicago Statement on Biblical Inerrancy" reads, "We affirm that God in His Work of inspiration utilized the distinctive personalities and literary styles of the writers whom He had chosen and prepared."[11] Frank Gaebelein sums up the matter when he confirms that "the original documents of the Bible were written by men, who, though permitted the exercises of their own personalities and literary talents, yet wrote under the control and guidance of the Spirit of God, the result being in every word of the original documents a perfect and errorless recording of the exact message which God desired to give to man."[12] By God's design,

---

6. Henry, *God, Revelation, and Authority*, 4:138–42.

7. Green, *2 Peter and Jude*, 102–3.

8. Moo, *2 Peter and Jude*, 85–86.

9. Vines and Shaddix, *Power in the Pulpit*, 51.

10. Stein, *A Basic Guide*, 28.

11. "The Chicago Statement," in Grudem, *Systematic Theology*, 1204.

12. Gaebelein, *Meaning of Inspiration*, 9.

the scriptural text throbs with human personality, yet possesses "truth, without any mixture of error, for its matter."[13]

Jesus Christ, God's ultimate revelation, is the most evident display of the anthropic nature of special revelation. In Hebrews 1:2, the author omits the definite article before the dative noun υἱῷ ("son") when writing that God "has spoken to us in His Son," which deliberately indicates Christ's superiority over prior revelation.[14] Just as the Nicene Creed (AD 325/381) affirms the full divinity of Christ, it is equally necessary that the Formulary of Chalcedon (AD 451) declares Jesus' full humanity.[15] In John 1:14, "the Word became flesh," the author's use of the term σάρξ ("flesh") can mean only that the eternally existent, divine *Logos* became truly human. The Bible indeed attributes to Jesus "the same sort of emotional and intellectual qualities that are found in other men."[16] Beyond the ontological reality of Christ's human nature, though, lies its epistemological function. Jesus "exegeted" (ἐξηγήσατο) the "very nature of God for the world" through his human existence on earth and, as such, "he left no question about his ability to communicate to humans an intimate understanding of the Father."[17] Thus, while God was—and is—directly present in Christ, the incarnation remains a revelation mediated through human personality.

Scripture nowhere maintains that preaching is in any way ontologically similar to Christ's incarnation or phenomenologically like the inspiration of the Bible, yet John Calvin's homiletical theology emphasizes that preaching is the continuation of the way that God—in his special revelation—has accommodated humanity's needs.[18] In the incarnation, "God so to speak makes himself little, in order to lower himself to our capacity; and Christ alone calms our consciences that they may dare intimately approach God."[19] In like manner, the words of God in Scripture "accommodate the knowledge of him to our slight capacity. To this he must descend far beneath his loftiness."[20] Calvin holds,

13. *Baptist Faith and Message*, 7.

14. Guthrie, *Letter to the Hebrews*, 63.

15. Creeds contained in Grudem, *Systematic Theology*, 1169. For discussion, see Olson, *Story of Christian Theology*, 154–55, 230–33.

16. Erickson, *Christian Theology*, 725.

17. Borchert, *John 1–11*, 119.

18. Battles, "God Was Accommodating Himself," 21–47.

19. Ibid., 38, quoting Calvin.

20. Calvin *Institutes* 1.13.1.

But how very wicked it is for us to yield less reverence to God's speaking because He lowers Himself to our ignorance! Let us know that it is for our sakes that the Lord prattles with us in Scripture in an awkward and common style. Whoever says that he is offended at such meanness or pleads it as an excuse for not subjecting himself to the Word of God is a liar. For he who cannot bear to embrace God when He is near him will certainly not fly away to Him above the clouds.[21]

Only in this manner does preaching become a continuation of Christ's incarnation or, for that matter, the inspiration of Scripture. Peter Adam identifies this connection between revelation and preaching in Calvin's thought: "God has accommodated to us in our weakness by providing us not only with Scripture but also with preachers and teachers."[22] Calvin makes much of the association:

He . . . provides for our weakness in that he prefers to address us in human fashion through interpreters in order to draw us to himself, rather than to thunder at us and drive us away.[23]

Therefore when the gospel is preached among us, God's applying himself in that way to our weakness is . . . how greatly he loves us in that he deals with us according to our own small capacity.[24]

God did not content himself to put forth the Holy Scripture that every man might study it, but he devised of his infinite goodness a second means to instruct us; he would have the doctrine that is therein contained preached and expounded to us. And for this end and purpose he has appointed shepherds in his church which have the office and charge of teaching. This aid God thought good to add because of our slowness. It was already very much that he had given us his word and caused it to be written that every one of us might read it and learn it. God showed himself herein very liberal toward us. But when we see he deals with us after our weakness and chews our morsels for us that we might digest them the better, in that he feeds us as little children, we shall never be able to excuse ourselves, unless we profit in his school.[25]

---

21. Calvin *The Gospel according to St. John 1–10* 3.12.

22. Adam, *Speaking God's Words*, 139.

23. Calvin *Institutes* 4.5.1.

24. Calvin, *Sermons on the Epistle to the Ephesians*, 376.

25. Calvin, *Sermons on the Epistles to Timothy and Titus*, 945.

God accommodates himself "completely to the theological, emotional, and spiritual needs of his people" by means of the incarnation, the Bible, and then the preacher.[26] For this reason, God has fixed the eldership as a permanent office in his church.[27] Elders ensure that God's truth, revealed propositionally through human personality, continues to be communicated. Paul makes it plain in his letter to Titus that a church without elders is incomplete (Titus 1:5). Moreover, while the elder's role includes pastoral tasks and congregational leadership, it must never exclude the preaching-teaching endeavor (1 Tim 3:2; 5:17).[28] Consequently, constructing "truth through personality" in an evangelical manner requires the person of the preacher to serve in an accommodating role. The preacher extends God's communicative mode of special revelation— through human personality—not ontologically or phenomenologically, but functionally.

THE PURPOSE OF PREACHING AND THE PERSON OF THE PREACHER

While evangelicals reject outright Phillips Brooks's homiletical goal of simply building character,[29] some of them still believe that it is "not possible to give a straightforward New Testament answer to the purpose of preaching."[30] Scripture, though, actually assigns to preaching a rather clear objective. In addition to God's glory as its ultimate end and the message of Jesus Christ as its primary content, the New Testament makes a direct correlation between preaching and the salvific efficaciousness of the gospel.[31] The apostle Paul offers a summary of his ministry in Colossians 1:24–29:

> Now I rejoice in my sufferings for your sake, and in my flesh I do
> my share on behalf of His body, which is the church, in filling up
> what is lacking in Christ's afflictions. Of this church I was made a

26. Adam, *Speaking God's Words*, 142.

27. Stott, *Between Two Worlds*, 116–17.

28. Separating teaching elders from ruling elders, which is common among Presbyterians, should be rejected on exegetical grounds. See Dever, *Nine Marks of a Healthy Church*, 55–59; Cowen, *Who Rules the Church?* 33–42.

29. Brooks, *Lectures*, 81, 136.

30. Adam, *Speaking God's Words*, 125.

31. For a helpful discussion of the goal of preaching, see Piper, *Supremacy of God in Preaching*, 17–36.

minister according to the stewardship from God bestowed on me for your benefit, so that I might fully carry out the preaching of the word of God, that is, the mystery which has been hidden from the past ages and generations, but has now been manifested to His saints, to whom God willed to make known what is the riches of the glory of this mystery among the Gentiles, which is Christ in you, the hope of glory. We proclaim Him, admonishing every man and teaching every man with all wisdom, so that we may present every man complete in Christ. For this purpose also I labor, striving according to His power, which mightily works within me.

In this passage, Paul explains his mission in view of the preeminence of Christ and his redeeming work (Col 1:13–23). With an eschatological thrust, Paul seeks to complete two tasks.[32] First, he will suffer for the sake of the gospel and the church. Second, he will "fully carry out the preaching of the word of God" (Col 1:25). Being divinely appointed as a minister, Paul delivers a previously veiled—but presently manifested—mystery: namely, "Christ in you, the hope of glory" (Col 1:27).

Paul's summary of his ministry ends with a more specific statement about his preaching's purpose. He proclaims Jesus to present every person as "complete" (τέλειος) in Christ—for rendering each believer "perfect," "whole," or "mature" (Col 1:28).[33] His use of the term τέλειος directly connects preaching to the salvific process, which he believes will be finalized at Christ's return.[34] Hence, Paul strives toward the same goal in preaching that Jesus' redemptive acts achieved. Earlier in the passage, Paul explains that Christ "has now reconciled you in his fleshly body through death, in order to present you before him holy and blameless and beyond reproach" (Col 1:22); this truth is the basis and purpose for his proclamation. If Paul's apostolic preaching constitutes a norm for all subsequent Christian preaching—and it does[35]—then preaching forms a means by which God conducts his saving work.

In Colossians 1:28, Paul not only displays the connection between his preaching and salvation, but additionally asserts the manner in which

---

32. Melick delineates the passage's eschatological nature as it employs terms and phrases like "affliction," "mystery," "administration," and "now revealed." Melick, *Philippians, Colossians, Philemon*, 237–41.

33. O'Brien, *Colossians, Philemon*, 89; BDAG 809.

34. Bruce, *Epistles to the Colossians*, 87.

35. Most evangelical preaching textbooks assume the normativeness of Paul's homiletic. See Shaddix, *Passion-Driven Sermon*, 9–62.

his preaching has its salvific effect. He obtains every person's completion in Christ by way of "admonishing" and "teaching"—terms that appear together again in Colossians 3:16. Admonishing (ϛουθετοῦντες) attempts "to correct the mind, to put right what is wrong, to improve the spiritual attitude."[36] Paul's use of the word indicates deliberate correction, in which the preacher gets "in the face" of another.[37] Likewise, teaching (διδάσκοντες) gives "from Scripture directions for Christian living."[38] He employs the term rarely and apparently for stressing forcefulness.[39] These terms—"admonishing" and "teaching"—illustrate that Paul did not accomplish his ministry by a superficial presentation of information, but rather "through warning and intensive teaching in pastoral situations."[40] In other words, Paul's work necessitates a person-to-person encounter.

According to Proverbs 27:17, "Iron sharpens iron, so one man sharpens another," and nothing less can be true in preaching. Paul's charge for Timothy to "preach the word" requires that he "reprove, rebuke, exhort, with great patience and instruction" (2 Tim 4:2). Calvin, in a sermon based on 2 Timothy 4:1–2, reinforces the point:

> And again Saint Paul shows that it is not enough to preach the Law of God and the promises, and what else so ever is contained in the holy Scripture, as though a man should teach in a school. But we must "improve, threaten, and exhort." If we leave it to men's choice to follow what is taught them, they will never move one foot. Therefore the doctrine of itself can profit nothing at all, unless it be confirmed by exhortations, and by threats, unless there be spurs to prick men withal. For beasts that are so wild and fierce, if they should be let alone to lie groveling in their slothfulness, it will be hard to make them profit in the end, and to go on in the way of salvation.[41]

While no evangelical denies the saving and sanctifying power of the Word as applied to the heart by the Holy Spirit (Heb 4:12–13), the person-to-person encounter of preaching remains a special, but typical,

---

36. *TDNT* 4:1019.

37. O'Brien, *Colossians, Philemon*, 88; Mohler, "Primacy of Preaching," 25.

38. *TDNT* 2:146.

39. O'Brien, *Colossians, Philemon*, 88.

40. Ibid.

41. Calvin, *Sermons on the Epistles to Timothy and Titus*, 947.

way by which God accomplishes his saving work. John Broadus poignantly explains how preaching the Bible, as opposed to merely reading it, marshals salvation:

> The great appointed means of spreading the good tidings of salvation through Christ is preaching. . . . When a man who is apt in teaching, whose soul is on fire with the truth which he trusts has saved him and hopes will save others, speaks to his fellow-men, face to face, eye to eye, and electric sympathies flash to and fro between him and his hearers . . . there is a power to move men, to influence character, life, destiny, such as no printed page can ever possess.[42]

D. Martyn Lloyd-Jones vigorously adds that the preacher stands to "do something to those people; he is there to produce results of various kinds. . . . He is there to deal with the whole person; and his preaching is meant to affect the whole person at the very center of life."[43]

Even in the present age of advanced technology and mass-media communication, John Piper points out that the Word of God still cries out for "expository exultation" displaying God's glory for the good of humanity.[44] Craig Larson concurs, "When our purpose is to reshape people into the image of Christ . . . nothing has greater potency than biblical preaching. . . . While other useful forms of ministry and media can present the Word of God, it is preaching that brings the full weight of the Word of God to bear on the soul and spirit."[45] As a result, "truth through personality," constructed evangelically, entails a person-to-person encounter in which the preacher confronts his hearers with the saving message of the gospel.

THE PERSON OF THE PREACHER
AND THE MESSAGE PREACHED

As discussed intermittently throughout this work, evangelical doctrines regarding the propositional, external character of special revelation and humankind's sinful nature inform and dictate the preacher's connection with God's Word. Brooks's persistent popularity and the trend toward

---

42. Broadus, *Treatise*, 17–18.

43. Lloyd-Jones, *Preaching and Preachers*, 53.

44. Piper, "Divine Majesty of the Word," 14.

45. Larson, "What Gives Preaching Its Power?" 32.

incarnational preaching models, though, require a clear delineation of the features of the relationship. Most evangelical preaching textbooks, even as they cite Brooks, maintain the notion of a preacher as a personal witness to a divine message—one who has received a message from the Lord, has allowed the message to penetrate his own life, and then bears testimony of that message to others.[46] Perhaps no homiletician has more precisely stated these essentials than Haddon Robinson. Although Robinson contends that no definition can capture the full range of the communicative dynamics of preaching, he nonetheless offers what he calls a "working definition":

> Expository preaching is the communication of a biblical concept, derived from and transmitted through a historical, grammatical, and literary study of a passage in its context, which the Holy Spirit first applies to the personality and experience of the preacher, then through the preacher, applies to the hearers.[47]

Hershael York supports Robinson's definition, and goes on to say that

> preaching is not from within the preacher, but it emanates from the text *through* the preacher. . . . We preach the Word to men and women, and we first let it grip our minds and hearts. . . . As we let God do something *to us*, he prepares to do something *through us* as his Word is preached.[48]

These categories—demarcated by Robinson's definition and echoed by York's comments—compose what is, fundamentally, the evangelical idea of "truth through personality."

The Message to the Preacher

York rightly observes that preaching originates from the scriptural text and not from within the preacher. Contemporary preaching indeed differs from New Testament apostolic preaching in the move away from a revelatory declarative function to an explanatory declarative function.[49]

---

46. For example, see Stott, *Between Two Worlds*, 116–33; McDill, *Moment of Truth*, 5–22; Chapell, *Christ-Centered Preaching*, 18–32; Quicke, *360-Degree Preaching*, 86–108; Vines and Shaddix, *Power in the Pulpit*, 24–31; Olford, *Anointed Expository Preaching*, 19–28, 232–35.

47. Robinson, *Biblical Preaching*, 21.

48. York and Decker, *Preaching with Bold Assurance*, 23.

49. Shaddix, *Passion-Driven Sermon*, 71–73.

The Bible, as God's inscripturated words, points to God's final Word—Jesus Christ. Due to the fact that the Word of Christ has credibility independent of the preacher (1 Cor 1:18–25; Phil 1:15–18), and because the gospel implicates the preacher as a sinner saved by grace, the preacher can do nothing to add to the reliability of the message or even commend himself as one qualified to preach it. Robinson remarks,

> Ultimately the authority behind expository preaching resides not in the preacher but in the biblical text. For that reason expositors deal largely with the explanation of Scripture. . . . Expositors may be respected for their exegetical abilities and their diligent preparation, but these qualities do not transform any of them into a Protestant pope who speaks *ex cathedra.*[50]

Therefore, preaching comes from preachers to whom the gospel has been sent and who have been sent by the gospel. The apostle Paul constantly labors to prove in his writings that his message and his missionary enterprise are not of his own devising. He received the gospel from God (Gal 1:11–12), was called to preach by God (1 Cor 1:17), and preaches as one sent from God (2 Cor 2:17). According to Paul, "For if I preach the gospel, I have nothing to boast of, for I am under compulsion; for woe is me if I do not preach the gospel" (1 Cor 9:16). D. Martyn Lloyd-Jones wisely remarks,

> What is the preacher? Well, obviously the preacher is a Christian like every other Christian. That is basic and an absolute essential. But he is something more than that, there is something further; and this is where this whole question of a call comes in. A preacher is not a Christian who decides to preach, he does not just decide to do it. . . . [T]here should also be a sense of constraint. This is surely the most crucial test. It means that you have the feeling that you can do nothing else.[51]

Therefore, a right concept of the preacher's relation to God's Word begins by acknowledging that the Word exists externally from him, comes to him definitively and propositionally in Scripture, and then sends him as a messenger.

---

50. Robinson, *Biblical Preaching*, 24.

51. Lloyd-Jones, *Preaching and Preachers*, 103–5.

The Message in the Preacher

Some preaching definitions concentrate on the external nature of the message and the human agency involved in delivering the message, but fail to highlight its impact on the preacher himself. For example, consider the definitions offered by Jerry Vines and Wayne McDill:

> [Preaching is] the oral communication of biblical truth by the Holy Spirit through a human personality to a given audience with the intent of enabling a positive response.[52]

> Christian preaching is an expression of the revelation of God through oral communication, declared by a God-called messenger, by the enabling of the Holy Spirit, containing a theological message from the biblical text, addressed to a particular audience in their situation, with the aim of calling the hearers to faith in God.[53]

By omitting the influence of the gospel on preachers, perhaps these definitions help them to avoid the error of preaching themselves (2 Cor 4:5). The very nature of the gospel, however, prevents the preacher from acting as merely a passive agent. The gospel alleges that all humans are sinful and need salvation, including the preacher. Paul indeed peppered his letters, and probably his preaching, with personal testimony of the work of the gospel in his own life. In Galatians 2:20, he proclaims, "I have been crucified with Christ; and it is no longer I who live, but Christ lives in me; and the life which I now live in the flesh I live by faith in the Son of God, who loved me and gave Himself up for me." True Christian preaching likewise resounds with personal testimony—not that the preacher must speak explicitly of his own conversion and sanctification, but the gospel constrains the preacher to preach in the same way that he lives: namely, "by faith in the Son of God." In fact, "to preach the cross of Christ and not to live out the cross for others effects a separation of witness: one's lived witness is separate from one's verbal witness."[54] Sinclair Ferguson summarizes the matter:

> In the last analysis, this is what preaching . . . is intended to produce: inner prostration of the hearts of our listeners through a consciousness of the presence and glory of God. This distinguishes authentic, biblical, expository preaching from any cheap

---

52. Vines and Shaddix, *Power in the Pulpit*, 27.

53. McDill, *Moment of Truth*, 20.

54. Resner, *Preacher and Cross*, 149.

substitute for it; it marks the difference between preaching about the Word of God and preaching the Word of God.[55]

This objective, though, occurs only after the preacher "has been laid bare before God by His Word. He, in turn, lays it bare in his ministry before those to whom he ministers."[56]

The Message through the Preacher

In 2 Corinthians 2:12–15, Paul describes the way the gospel message is presented through him:

> Now when I came to Troas for the gospel of Christ and when a door was opened for me in the Lord, I had no rest for my spirit, not finding Titus my brother; but taking my leave of them, I went on to Macedonia. But thanks be to God, who always leads us in triumph in Christ, and manifests through us the sweet aroma of the knowledge of Him in every place. For we are fragrance of Christ to God among those who are being saved and among those who are perishing; to the one an aroma from death to death, to the other an aroma from life to life.

While Brooks's oft-cited contention that the gospel should come "through" the preacher and not "over" the preacher focuses more on the preacher himself,[57] the apostle Paul's perception of the message coming "through" the messenger aims more squarely at its recipients. Paul Barnett observes,

> [T]his manifestation of Christ is not located in Paul's *person*—as if by some kind of incarnation—but *in his gospel ministry*. This is clear from the immediate context, which shows that Paul is referring to his reason for coming to Troas, namely, "for the gospel of Christ" (2 Cor 2:12). It is by Paul . . . that God manifests the knowledge of Christ. It is not in his person alone, but through Christ crucified and risen whom he proclaims and whose sufferings he replicates, that Paul manifests the knowledge of Christ. The proclamation of Christ is like a strong fragrance, unseen but yet powerful, impinging on all who encounter Paul in his sufferings as he preaches Christ wherever he goes. In the victory parade metaphor of this verse, the apostle is God's captive, whom

55. Ferguson, "Preaching to the Heart," 196.

56. Ibid., 195.

57. Brooks, *Lectures*, 8.

God leads about spreading the knowledge of Christ—incense-like—by means of the proclamation of Christ.[58]

In his apostolic model, the gospel's coming "through" Paul serves the purpose of "spreading the knowledge of Christ." Contemporary preaching, therefore—as Stott maintains—exists "to enable God's revealed truth to flow out of the Scriptures into the lives of men and women today."[59] It seems that such a flow carries implications for both presentation and application in preaching.

Personal presence and style matters become vital issues in the event of preaching because the gospel makes demands on its preacher.[60] Paul confesses, "I was with you in fear and trembling" (1 Cor 2:3). A personal presentation, which matches the message preached, represents the Christian preaching standard. Preachers must avoid arrogance and self-promotion at any level, surrender personal tastes, accommodate cultural norms for the advance of the gospel (1 Cor 9:20–23), and flee especially from aloof eloquence when preaching. According to Broadus, "In all speaking, especially in preaching, naturalness, genuineness, even though awkward, is really more effective . . . than the most elegant artificiality."[61] D. Martyn Lloyd-Jones agrees:

> A man prepares a message and, having prepared it, he may be pleased and satisfied with the arrangement and order of the thoughts and certain forms of expression. . . . [H]e may well be excited and moved by that and especially when he preaches the sermon. But it may be entirely of the flesh and have nothing at all to do with spiritual matters. Every preacher knows exactly what this means. . . . You can be carried away by your own eloquence and by the very thing you yourself are doing and not by the truth at all.[62]

In other words, a Christian preacher cannot simply regurgitate biblical data, clone his homiletical hero, or squeeze himself into an artificial persona when he stands to preach. In fact, Vines proposes that, the moment a preacher tries to be someone else when he preaches, "He ceases to

58. Barnett, *Second Epistle to the Corinthians,* 151–52.

59. Stott, *Between Two Worlds,* 138.

60. Resner, *Preacher and Cross,* 112.

61. Broadus, *Treatise,* 14.

62. Lloyd-Jones, *Studies in the Sermon on the Mount,* 2:266.

preach."[63] Obviously, a preacher should aim to learn all that he can from skilled homileticians and attempt to improve his delivery. Allowing the gospel to come through a preacher, though, means that the preaching cannot be severed from the person doing it.[64] Chapell contends, "Congregations ask no more and expect no less of a preacher than truth expressed in a manner consistent with the personality of the preacher and reflective of the import of the message."[65]

As much as the manner of presentation remains a significant issue in Christian preaching, it does not eclipse the matter of the material presented. In Stott's bridge-building metaphor, preaching relates "God's unchanging Word to our ever-changing world."[66] In an insightful article, York and Scott Blue hold that the preacher "does not need to *make* Scripture relevant. He must, however, *demonstrate* its relevance; that is, he must appreciate the task of 'transferring a relevant message from the past to the present.'"[67] Consequently, they recommend application as an "essential component" of preaching, and they define application as

> the process whereby the expositor takes a biblical truth of the text and applies it to the lives of his audience, proclaiming why it is relevant for their lives, practically showing how it should affect their lives, and passionately encouraging them to make necessary changes in their lives in a manner congruent with the original intent of the author.[68]

Some disdain the idea of sermon application, believing that it portrays the Bible as an antiquated document or undermines its authority.[69] Paul's charge for Timothy to "preach the word," though, includes demands that he "reprove, rebuke, exhort, with great patience and instruction" (2 Tim 4:2)—terms that infer some sort of application of the message to the hearers' lives. In fact, the Bible's apex statement concerning its own origination and inspiration comes with an affirmation that all Scripture is "profitable for teaching, for reproof, for correction,

---

63. Vines and Shaddix, *Power in the Pulpit*, 26.

64. Robinson, *Biblical Preaching*, 25–27.

65. Chapell, *Christ-Centered Preaching*, 313.

66. Stott, *Between Two Worlds*, 144.

67. York and Blue, "Is Application Necessary?" 78; Greidanus, *Modern Preacher and the Ancient Text*, 159.

68. York and Blue, "Is Application Necessary?" 74–76.

69. Ibid., 70–71; MacArthur, "Moving from Exegesis to Exposition," 300.

for training in righteousness" (2 Tim 3:16)—again explicitly claiming that scriptural truth should be applied to life situations. Hence, sermon application is not an issue adjacent to preaching, but is one of preaching's necessary facets and part of an evangelical construction of "truth through personality."

CONCLUSION

When conceived as an evangelical axiom for Christian preaching, "truth through personality" acknowledges—with joy—that God has spoken his eternal truth in a way humans can comprehend: through human personality. Preaching, while not in any way a replication of the incarnation or the event of inspiration, nonetheless extends God's communicative mode in special revelation by means of accommodation. Preachers exist to chew the food, so to speak, for dispensing the vital spiritual nutrition of God's Word.

Preaching, like Christ's work and God's Word, has a salvific aim. As a result, when preachers explain, teach, and urge hearers to believe and embrace biblical truths, "The Word of God achieves its purpose, and this is one of the normal ways in which God brings his Word to human beings."[70] The nature of the gospel, though, defines the preacher's relationship to the message preached. The message must come to the preacher from Scripture; impact his heart and life; and pass from him to the audience. Additionally, an evangelical concept of "truth through personality" requires—on a theological level—that the manner of personal presentation be consistent with the gospel and that the gospel be applied to the auditors' lives. Hopefully, evangelicals have this construction in mind when they cite "truth through personality," even if they erroneously endorse the phrase as coined by Phillips Brooks.

---

70. Adam, *Speaking God's Words*, 118.

6

Summary and Conclusion

Iɴ *A Hɪsᴛᴏʀʏ ᴏꜰ Pʀᴇᴀᴄʜɪɴɢ*, Ralph G. Turnbull contends that Phillips
Brooks "gave the church the imperishable idea about preaching"[1] when
he presented his "truth through personality" concept. Indeed, during
the thirteen decades since Brooks coined the phrase, it has been quoted
incessantly and utilized so widely that Wiersbe maintains, "Everything
useful written on homiletics in America in the last century is in one
way or another a footnote to Phillips Brooks."[2] Undoubtedly—except for
perhaps a few very extreme ideologies that cast the preacher merely as a
herald—Christian preaching, by its nature, cannot escape being "truth
through personality." Brooks himself captured the concept's universal
scope in his *Lectures on Preaching*: "The truest truth, the most authoritative statement of God's will, communicated in any other way than
through personality of brother man to men is not preached truth."[3]

The axiomatic nature of "truth through personality," however, has
led many evangelicals to endorse Phillips Brooks and to refer to his slogan uninhibitedly and without proper reflection. He lived during a time
when Darwinian evolution and higher biblical criticism were challeng-
ing Christian foundations. He—along with other Protestants—sought
to make Christianity believable again by jettisoning traditional doctrinal
formulations and embracing a more subjective, experiential, and theologically ambiguous form of faith, based mostly on romanticism. Having
cut his philosophical and spiritual teeth on romantic authors like Horace
Bushnell and Samuel Taylor Coleridge, Brooks gleaned their heightened
anthropology and concluded that all humans are—eternally—God's
children.

1. Turnbull, *From the Close of the Nineteenth Century*, 111.
2. Wiersbe, "Preacher of Truth and Life," 7.
3. Brooks, *Lectures*, 7.

Such anthropological convictions wielded massive ramifications concerning his soteriological views to the point that he denied original sin, mitigated any substitutionary component in Christ's atonement, and reduced conversion to nurturing character. Yet, Brooks kept his romanticism within the Christian realm by appealing to Jesus' incarnation and placing it at the very center of his theology. He indeed employed the incarnation to support his anthropology by asserting that "Christ was what man had felt in his soul that he might be. Christ did what man's heart had always told him that it was in his humanity to do."[4] The incarnation serves in his thought as the model for anthropology, and this very man-centered construct forms the axis around which all his convictions revolve. For him, revelation occurs incarnationally within personalities; God may be thought of as the superlative of his image found in humanity; and salvation consists solely in a person coming to realize that he or she is a child of God—a miniature incarnation.

From Brooks's romantic and incarnational theology emerged a homiletic—a concept of "truth through personality"—that emphasized the personal, not propositional, nature of truth; the transfer of personal truth in a manner directly analogous to the incarnation; and the goal of preaching as the perfection of those who already are "full of the suggestion of God."[5] Although Brooks always used evangelical terminology and engaged his preaching with evangelical fervency, he nevertheless formulated "truth through personality" in a manner decidedly inconsistent with evangelical convictions. He dismissed external, propositional revelation, thus making the Bible into merely a book of catchphrases for launching into one's own speculations. His idea that preaching is the "continuation, out to the minutest ramifications" of Christ's incarnation presents an ontological relationship between the preacher and God's Word that— while permissible within his romantic anthropology—borders on heresy. Finally, Brooks's focus on building character as preaching's goal places too high a demand on the preacher's own character, and therefore introduces a persuasive model that is ultimately incompatible with the sinners-saved-by-grace nature of the scriptural gospel (Eph 2:1–10).

Evangelicals, though, can helpfully employ the phrase, "truth through personality," by supporting the concept with evangelical doctrines. A biblical anthropology confessing humanity's special—yet fall-

4. Brooks, *Visions and Tasks*, 282.
5. Brooks, *Lectures*, 259.

en—status recognizes the need for external, propositional revelation that, in turn, expresses the reality of salvation by faith in Jesus Christ's redemptive work. God has spoken, and his special revelation arrives in anthropic form, but no preacher can ever replicate God's revelatory activity—either in the inspiration of Scripture or in Christ's incarnation. Preaching, rather, extends the communicative mode of special revelation by means of accommodation—condescending to human weakness. A proper and evangelical construction of "truth through personality" insists that a preacher exists as a personal witness to a divine message. The message is external to him, but it comes to him in Scripture; it radically changes him; and—as he lives and preaches in a manner consistent with the message—it emanates from him to others. Ultimately, in the person-to-person confrontation of preaching, the preacher aims to present his hearers as "complete in Christ" (Col 1:28), and God accomplishes the salvific effects of the gospel.

In light of the serious deficiencies inherent in Brooks's construction of "truth through personality," evangelicals ought not refer to his preaching definition without clarification. Undoubtedly, if evangelicals want to employ "truth through personality" as an axiom in their preaching discussions—and clearly they may—then they must plainly delineate their intentions. First of all, evangelical homileticians should explain the proper distance between the preacher and God's Word by reiterating special revelation's external, propositional, and *sui generis* nature. They should invoke Christ's incarnation only in a way that illustrates some of preaching's practical necessities—like authenticity and relevance—but not as a theological ground or ontological model for preaching. Second, evangelical preachers should allow God's Word to penetrate into their hearts and engage their hearers in a person-to-person confrontation, but they must present themselves in a manner consistent with their message—as sinners saved solely by grace. In sum, Brooks's famous phrase, "truth through personality," can remain the "imperishable idea about preaching" only if it is constructed upon the indestructible truth of the message preached (Isa 40:8).

Bibliography

Abbott, Edward. *Phillips Brooks: A Memory of the Bishop, an Impression of the Man, a Study of the Preacher, with the Digest of His Theological Teachings.* Cambridge, MA: Powell, 1900.

Abbott, Lyman. "The Supernatural." *The Outlook* 9 (1888) 583.

Adam, Peter. *Speaking God's Words: A Practical Theology of Preaching.* Leicester, England: Inter-Varsity, 1996.

Akin, Daniel L., editor. *A Theology for the Church.* Nashville: B&H, 2007.

Albright, Raymond W. *Focus on Infinity: A Life of Phillips Brooks.* New York: Macmillan, 1961.

Allen, Alexander V. G. *Life and Letters of Phillips Brooks.* 3 vols. New York: E. P. Dutton, 1901.

———. *Phillips Brooks: Memories of His Life with Extracts from His Letters and Notebooks.* New York: E. P. Dutton, 1907.

Anderson, R. Dean, Jr. *Glossary of Greek Rhetorical Terms Connected to Methods of Argumentation, Figures, and Tropes from Anaximenes to Quintilian.* Leuven, Belgium: Peeters, 2000.

Aristotle. *The Rhetoric of Aristotle.* Translated by Lane Cooper. Englewood Cliffs, NJ: Prentice-Hall, 1932.

Augustine. *On Christian Doctrine.* Translated by D. W. Robertson Jr. New York: Liberal Arts, 1958.

Baird, Robert. *Religion in America.* New York: Harper, 1844.

The Baptist Faith and Message. Nashville: Lifeway, 2000.

Barnette, Paul. *The Second Epistle to the Corinthians.* The New International Commentary on the New Testament. Grand Rapids: Eerdmans, 1997.

Barth, Karl. *Church Dogmatics.* Edited by G. W. Bromiley and T. F. Torrance. Vol. 1, *The Doctrine of the Word of God.* Pt. 2. Translated by G. T. Thomas and Harold Knight. Edinburgh: T & T Clark, 1956.

Battles, Ford Lewis. "God Was Accommodating Himself to Human Capacity." *Interpretation* 31 (1977) 21–47.

Bauer, Walter. *A Greek-English Lexicon of the New Testament and Other Early Christian Literature.* Second edition. Translated by William F. Arndt and F. Wilbur Gingrich. Chicago: University of Chicago Press, 1979.

Bayer, Oswald. *Theology the Lutheran Way.* Translated by Jeffrey G. Silcock and Mark C. Mattes. Grand Rapids: Eerdmans, 2007.

Bebbington, David W. "Evangelicalism in Its Settings: The British and American Movements since 1940." In *Evangelicalism: Comparative Studies of Popular Protestantism in North America, the British Isles, and Beyond, 1700—1900,* 365–88. New York: Oxford University Press, 1994.

——. *Evangelicalism in Modern Britain: A History from the 1730s to the 1980s.* Winchester, MA: Allen & Unwin, 1989.

Beecher, Lyman. *The Faith Once Delivered to the Saints.* Boston: Crocker and Brewster, 1824.

Bloesch, Donald G. *Essentials of Evangelical Theology.* San Francisco: Harper & Row, 1978.

——. *Holy Scripture: Revelation, Inspiration, and Interpretation.* Downers Grove, IL: InterVarsity, 1994.

Bonhoeffer, Dietrich. *Worldly Preaching: Lectures on Homiletics.* Edited by Clyde Fant. Nashville: Thomas Nelson, 1975.

Borchert, Gerald. *John 1–11.* The New American Commentary. Vol. 25A. Nashville: Broadman & Holman, 1996.

Boyce, James Petigru. *Abstract of Systematic Theology.* Philadelphia: American Baptist, 1887. Reprint, Hanford, CA: den Dulk Christian Foundation.

Brastow, Lewis O. *The Modern Pulpit: A Study of Homiletic Sources and Characteristics.* New York: Macmillan, 1906.

——. *Representative Modern Preachers.* New York: Hodder & Stoughton, 1904.

Britton, Joseph. "The Breadth of Orthodoxy: On Phillips Brooks." In *One Lord, One Faith, One Baptism: Studies in Christian Ecclesiality and Ecumenism in Honor of J. Robert Wright,* edited by Marsha L. Dutton and Patrick Terrell Gray, 144–62. Grand Rapids: Eerdmans, 2006.

Broadus, John A. *A Treatise on the Preparation and Delivery of Sermons.* New York: A. C. Armstrong and Son, 1895.

Brooks, Phillips. *Alexander Hamilton Vinton: A Memorial Sermon.* Boston: A. Williams, 1881.

——. "Authority and Conscience." In *Essays and Addresses: Religious, Literary, and Social,* 105–18. New York: E. P. Dutton, 1895.

——. *The Battle of Life: And Other Sermons.* New York: E. P. Dutton, 1910.

——. "The Candle of the Lord." In *The Candle of the Lord: And Other Sermons,* 1–21. New York: E. P. Dutton, 1903.

——. "The Conqueror from Edom." In *The Purpose and Use of Comfort: And Other Sermons,* 37–56. New York: E. P. Dutton, 1910.

——. "The Duty of the Business Man." In *Phillips Brooks's Addresses,* 70–95. Boston: Charles E. Brown, 1893.

——. *Essays and Addresses: Religious, Literary, and Social.* New York: E. P. Dutton, 1895.

——. "The Eternal Humanity." In *The Battle of Life: And Other Sermons,* 310–26. New York: E. P. Dutton, 1910.

——. "The Fire and the Calf." In *Sermons Preached in English Churches,* 43–64. New York: E. P. Dutton, 1883.

——. "First Sunday in Lent." In *Sermons for the Principal Festivals and Fasts of the Church Year,* 130–49. New York: E. P. Dutton, 1910.

——. "Fourth Sunday in Advent." In *Sermons for the Principal Festivals and Fasts of the Church Year,* 184–95. New York: E. P. Dutton, 1910.

——. "The Giant with the Wounded Heel." In *Twenty Sermons,* 93–109. New York: E. P. Dutton, 1887.

——. "Good Friday." In *Sermons for the Principal Festivals and Fasts of the Church Year,* 259–68. New York: E. P. Dutton, 1910.

———. "Heresy." In *Essays and Addresses: Religious, Literary, and Social*, 7–19. New York: E. P. Dutton, 1895.

———. *The Influence of Jesus*. New York: E. P. Dutton, 1888.

———. "The Knowledge of God." In *Twenty Sermons*, 280–96. New York: E. P. Dutton, 1887.

———. *Lectures on Preaching*. New York: E. P. Dutton, 1907.

———. *The Light of the World: And Other Sermons*. New York: E. P. Dutton, 1890.

———. "The Light of the World." In *The Light of the World: And Other Sermons*, 1–23. New York: E. P. Dutton, 1890.

———. "Literature and Life." In *Essays and Addresses: Religious, Literary, and Social*, 454–81. New York: E. P. Dutton, 1895.

———. "Living Epistles." In *Seeking Life: And Other Sermons*, 110–25. New York: E. P. Dutton, 1904.

———. "The Manliness of Christ." In *The Candle of the Lord: And Other Sermons*, 253–69. New York: E. P. Dutton, 1903.

———. *The Mystery of Iniquity: And Other Sermons*. London: Macmillan, 1893.

———. "The Mystery of Iniquity." In *The Mystery of Iniquity: And Other Sermons*, 1–17. London: Macmillan, 1893.

———. "The Nearness of God." In *Seeking Life: And Other Sermons*, 37–56. New York: E. P. Dutton, 1904.

———. "Need of Enthusiasm for Humanity." In *National Needs and Remedies*, 296–312. New York: Baker & Taylor, 1890.

———. "The New and Greater Miracle." In *The Light of the World: And Other Sermons*, 24–39. New York: E. P. Dutton, 1890.

———. "New Experiences." In *The Light of the World: And Other Sermons*, 287–305. New York: E. P. Dutton, 1890.

———. "The New Theism." In *Essays and Addresses: Religious, Literary, and Social*, 150–61. New York: E. P. Dutton, 1895.

———. "The Opening of the Eyes." In *The Light of the World: And Other Sermons*, 194–215. New York: E. P. Dutton, 1890.

———. "Orthodoxy." In *Essays and Addresses: Religious, Literary, and Social*, 183–97. New York: E. P. Dutton, 1895.

———. *Phillips Brooks Year Book*. New York: E. P. Dutton, 1894.

———. "The Pulpit and Popular Skepticism." In *Essays and Addresses: Religious, Literary, and Social*, 61–81. New York: E. P. Dutton, 1895.

———. "The Purposes of Scholarship." In *Essays and Addresses: Religious, Literary, and Social*, 247–72. New York: E. P. Dutton, 1895.

———. "Second Sunday in Advent." In *Sermons for the Principal Festivals and Fasts of the Church Year*, 18–34. New York: E. P. Dutton, 1910.

———. *Seeking Life: And Other Sermons*. New York: E. P. Dutton, 1904.

———. *Sermons for the Principal Festivals and Fasts of the Church Year*. New York: E. P. Dutton, 1910.

———. "The Spiritual Man." In *The Law of Growth: And Other Sermons*, 294–310. New York: E. P. Dutton, 1903.

———. "Sunday after Christmas." In *Sermons for the Principal Festivals and Fasts of the Church Year*, 97–109. New York: E. P. Dutton, 1910.

———. "The Transfiguration of Christ." In *The Consolations of God: Great Sermons of Phillips Brooks*, edited by Ellen Wilbur, 118–28. Grand Rapids: Eerdmans, 2003.

————. "Trinity Sunday." In *Sermons for the Principal Festivals and Fasts of the Church Year*, 318–35. New York: E. P. Dutton, 1910.

————. *Visions and Tasks: And Other Sermons*. New York: E. P. Dutton, 1910.

————. "Why Could We Not Cast Him Out?" In *Sermons Preached in English Churches*, 179–99. New York: E. P. Dutton, 1883.

Brown, H. C., Jr., H. Gordon Clinard, Jesse J. Northcutt, and Al Fasol. *Steps to the Sermon: An Eight-Step Plan for Preaching with Confidence*. Revised edition. Nashville: Broadman & Holman, 1996.

Bruce, F. F. *The Epistles to the Colossians, to Philemon, and to the Ephesians*. The New International Commentary on the New Testament. Grand Rapids: Eerdmans, 1984.

Buell, Lawrence. "The Unitarian Movement and the Art of Preaching in Nineteenth-Century America." *American Quarterly* 24 (1972) 166–90.

Bullinger, Henry. *The Decades of Henry Bullinger*. Edited by Thomas Harding. Cambridge: Cambridge University Press, 1849.

Bushnell, Horace. *God in Christ*. New York: Scribner, 1876.

Calvin, John. *Commentary on the Book of the Prophet Isaiah*. Translated by William Pringle. Edinburgh: Calvin Translation Society. Reprint, Grand Rapids: Baker, 1996.

————. *The Gospel according to St. John 1–10*. Edited by David W. Torrance and Thomas F. Torrance. Translated by T. H. L. Parker. Grand Rapids: Eerdmans, 1959.

————. *Institutes of the Christian Religion*. Edited by John T. McNeill. Translated by Ford Lewis Battles. Library of Christian Classics, vols. 20–21. Philadelphia: Westminster, 1960.

————. *Sermons on the Epistle to the Ephesians*. Translated by Arthur Golding. 1577. Reprint, Edinburgh: Banner of Truth, 1973.

————. *Sermons on the Epistles to Timothy and Titus: Sixteenth—Seventeenth Century Facsimile Editions*. Translated by L. T. 1579. Reprint, Edinburgh: Banner of Truth, 1983.

Chapell, Bryan. *Christ-Centered Preaching: Redeeming the Expository Sermon*. Second edition. Grand Rapids: Baker, 2005.

Chesebrough, David B. *Phillips Brooks: Pulpit Eloquence*. Westport, CT: Greenwood, 2001.

"The Chicago Statement on Biblical Inerrancy." In Wayne Grudem, *Systematic Theology: An Introduction to Biblical Doctrine*, 1203–5. Grand Rapids: Zondervan, 1994.

Chorley, E. Clowes. *Men and Movements in the American Episcopal Church*. New York: Scribner, 1946.

Coleridge, Samuel Taylor. *Aids to Reflection*. London: Hurst, Chance, 1831.

————. *Confessions of an Inquiring Spirit*. London: Edward Moxon, 1863.

Copleston, Frederick. *Modern Philosophy: Empiricism, Idealism, and Pragmatism in Britain and America*. Vol. 8 of *A History of Philosophy*. New York: Doubleday, 1967.

Cosgrove, Charles H., and W. Dow Edgerton. *In Other Words: Incarnational Translation for Preaching*. Grand Rapids: Eerdmans, 2007.

Cowen, Gerald P. *Who Rules the Church? Examining Congregational Leadership and Church Government*. Nashville: Broadman & Holman, 2003.

Craddock, Fred B. *As One without Authority*. Third edition. Nashville: Abingdon, 1979.

————. "Occasion-Text-Sermon: A Case Study." *Interpretation* 35 (1981) 59–71.

Dabney, Robert L. *Sacred Rhetoric.* Richmond, VA: Presbyterian Committee, 1870.

Daniels, W. H., editor. *Moody: His Words, Work, and Workers.* New York: Nelson & Phillips, 1877.

Dargan, Edwin Charles. *A History of Preaching.* 2 vols. New York: George H. Doran, 1905.

Davis, Ozora. "A Quarter-Century of American Preaching." *The Journal of Religion* 6 (1926) 135–53.

Dever, Mark E. *Nine Marks of a Healthy Church.* Fourth edition. Washington, DC: 9Marks, 2005.

DiCicco, Mario M. *Paul's Use of Ethos, Pathos, and Logos in 2 Corinthians 10–13.* Lewiston, NY: Edwin Mellen, 1995.

Drake, Francis S. "Vinton, Alexander Hamilton." In *Dictionary of American Biography*, 943. Boston: James R. Osgood and Company, 1872.

Dulles, Avery. *Models of Revelation.* Maryknoll, NY: Orbis, 1992.

Ensley, Francis Gerald. "Phillips Brooks and the Incarnation." *Religion in Life* 3 (1951) 350–61.

Erickson, Millard J. *Christian Theology.* Second edition. Grand Rapids: Baker, 1998.

Fant, Clyde. *Preaching for Today.* Revised edition. San Francisco: Harper & Row, 1987.

Farmer, Herbert H. *The Servant of the Word.* London: Nisbet, 1941.

Ferguson, Sinclair. "Preaching to the Heart." In *Feed My Sheep: A Passionate Plea for Preaching*, edited by Don Kistler, 190–217. Morgan, PA: Soli Deo Gloria, 2002.

Fung, Ronald Y. K. *The Epistle to the Galatians.* The New International Commentary on the New Testament. Grand Rapids: Eerdmans, 1988.

Gaebelein, Frank E. *The Meaning of Inspiration.* Chicago: InterVarsity, 1950.

George, Timothy. *Galatians.* The New American Commentary, vol. 30. Nashville: Broadman & Holman, 1994.

Green, Michael. *2 Peter and Jude.* Revised edition. Tyndale New Testament Commentaries, vol. 18. Grand Rapids: Eerdmans, 1987.

Greidanus, Sidney. *The Modern Preacher and the Ancient Text: Interpreting and Preaching Biblical Literature.* Grand Rapids: Eerdmans, 1988.

Grenz, Stanley J. *Renewing the Center: Evangelical Theology in a Post-Theological Era.* Grand Rapids: Baker, 2000.

———. *Theology for the Community of God.* Nashville: Broadman & Holman, 1994.

Grudem, Wayne. *Systematic Theology: An Introduction to Biblical Doctrine.* Grand Rapids: Zondervan, 1994.

Guelzo, Allen. "Ritualism, Romanism, and Rebellion." *Anglican and Episcopal History* 62 (1993) 553.

Gundry, Stanley N. *Love Them In: The Life and Theology of D. L. Moody.* Chicago: Moody, 1999.

Guthrie, Donald. *The Letter to the Hebrews: An Introduction and Commentary.* Tyndale New Testament Commentaries, vol. 15. Grand Rapids: Eerdmans, 1983.

Hankins, Barry. *American Evangelicals: A Contemporary History of a Mainstream Religious Movement.* New York: Rowman & Littlefield, 2008.

Harp, Gillis J. *Brahmin Prophet: Phillips Brooks and the Path of Liberal Protestantism.* New York: Rowman & Littlefield, 2003.

———. "The Young Phillips Brooks: A Reassessment." *Journal of Ecclesiastical History* 4 (1998) 652–67.

Heisler, Greg. *Spirit-Led Preaching: The Holy Spirit's Role in Sermon Preparation and Delivery*. Nashville: B&H, 2007.

Helm, Paul. *The Divine Revelation*. New York: Image, 1985.

Henry, Carl F. H. *God, Revelation, and Authority*. Vol. 1, *God Who Speaks and Shows: Preliminary Considerations*. Waco, TX: Word, 1976. Reprint, Wheaton, IL: Crossway, 1999.

———. *God, Revelation, and Authority*. Vol. 3, *God Who Speaks and Shows: Fifteen Theses, Part Two*. Waco, TX: Word, 1976. Reprint, Wheaton, IL: Crossway, 1999.

———. *God, Revelation, and Authority*. Vol. 4, *God Who Speaks and Shows: Fifteen Theses, Part Three*. Dallas: Word, 1979. Reprint, Wheaton, IL: Crossway, 1999.

Hicks, Peter. *Evangelicals and Truth*. Leicester, England: Apollos, 1958.

———. *The Journey So Far: Philosophy through the Ages*. Grand Rapids: Zondervan, 2003.

Hodge, Charles. *Anthropology*. Vol. 2 of *Systematic Theology*. New York: Scribner, 1873. Reprint, Peabody, MA: Hendrickson, 1999.

Hoekema, Anthony A. *Created in God's Image*. Grand Rapids: Eerdmans, 1986.

Hogan, Lucy Lind, and Robert Reid. *Connecting with the Congregation: Rhetoric and the Art of Preaching*. Nashville: Abingdon, 1999.

Howden, William D. "'The Pulpit Leads the World': Preachers and Preaching in Nineteenth-Century America." *American Transcendental Quarterly* 14 (2000) 169–72.

Huffman, John A., Jr. "The Role of Preaching in Ministry." In *The Pastor's Guide to Effective Preaching*, 35–46. Kansas City, MO: Beacon Hill, 2003.

Hyde, Thomas Alexander. "The Rev. Phillips Brooks." *The Arena* 1 (1890) 716–17.

Jones, Edgar DeWitt. *The Royalty of the Pulpit*. New York: Harper & Row, 1951.

Kennedy, George. *Classical Rhetoric & Its Christian & Secular Tradition from Ancient to Modern Times*. Second edition. Chapel Hill: The University of North Carolina Press, 1999.

Larson, Craig Brian. "What Gives Preaching Its Power?" *Leadership* 2 (2004) 30–32.

Lawrence, William. *Life of Phillips Brooks*. New York: Harper, 1930.

———. *Phillips Brooks*. Boston: Houghton Mifflin, 1903.

———. *Phillips Brooks: A Study*. New York: Houghton Mifflin, 1903.

Lea, Thomas D., and Hayne P. Griffin Jr. *1, 2 Timothy, Titus*. The New American Commentary, vol. 34. Nashville: Broadman, 1992.

Lischer, Richard. *Theories of Preaching: Selected Readings in the Homiletical Tradition*. Durham, NC: Labyrinth, 1987.

Litfin, Duane. *St. Paul's Theology of Proclamation: 1 Corinthians 1–4 and Greco-Roman Rhetoric*. Cambridge: Cambridge University Press, 1994.

Lloyd, J. T. *Life of Henry Ward Beecher*. London: Tyne, 1881.

Lloyd-Jones, D. Martyn. *Authority*. London: Inter-Varsity, 1958.

———. *Preaching and Preachers*. Grand Rapids: Zondervan, 1971.

———. *Studies in the Sermon on the Mount*. Grand Rapids: Eerdmans, 1960.

Long, Frederick J. *Ancient Rhetoric and Paul's Apology*. Cambridge: Cambridge University Press, 2004.

Long, Thomas G. *The Witness of Preaching*. Second edition. Louisville: Westminster/John Knox, 2005.

MacArthur, John, Jr. "Moving from Exegesis to Exposition." In *Rediscovering Expository Preaching*, edited by Richard Mayhew, 288–302. Dallas: Word, 1992.

Machen, J. Gresham. *Christianity & Liberalism.* New York: Macmillan, 1923.

MacLeod, Donald. *The Person of Christ.* Downers Grove, IL: InterVarsity, 1998.

Maurice, Frederick Denison. *The Kingdom of Christ.* 2 vols. London: Gilbert & Rivington, 1842.

May, Henry F. *Protestant Churches in Industrial America.* New York: Harper, 1949.

McDill, Wayne V. *The Moment of Truth: A Guide to Effective Sermon Delivery.* Nashville: Broadman & Holman, 1999.

McIlvaine, Charles P. *The Work of Preaching Christ.* Boston: Gospel Book & Tract Depository, 1871.

McLeod, Norman Bruce. "Levels of Relevance in Preaching: A Historical Study of the Communication of the Word to the World by a Witness, with special attention to the principles of interpretation used in the preaching of Phillips Brooks from 1859 to 1892." ThD diss., Union Theological Seminary, 1960.

———. "The Preaching of Phillips Brooks: A Study of Relevance versus Eternal Truth." *Religion in Life* 1 (1964–65) 50–67.

McLoughlin, William G. Introduction to *The American Evangelicals, 1800—1900,* 1–27. New York: Harper & Row, 1968.

Melick, Richard R., Jr. *Philippians, Colossians, Philemon.* The New American Commentary, vol. 32. Nashville: Broadman, 1991.

Meuser, Fred W. "Luther as Preacher of the Word of God." In *The Cambridge Companion to Martin Luther,* edited by Donald K. McKim, 136–48. Cambridge: Cambridge University Press, 2003.

Minyard, Alfred Benson. "The Theology of Phillips Brooks." PhD diss., Boston University, 1957.

Mitchell, Margaret M. *Paul and the Rhetoric of Reconciliation: An Exegetical Investigation of the Language and Composition of 1 Corinthians.* Louisville: Westminster/John Knox, 1991.

Mohler, R. Albert, Jr. "The Primacy of Preaching." In *Feed My Sheep: A Passionate Plea for Preaching,* edited by Don Kistler, 1–32. Morgan, PA: Soli Deo Gloria, 2002.

———. "Reformist Evangelicalism: A Center without a Circumference." In *A Confessing Theology for Postmodern Times,* edited by Michael S. Horton, 131–52. Wheaton, IL: Crossway, 2000.

———. "A Theology of Preaching." In *Handbook of Contemporary Preaching,* edited by Michael Diduit, 13–20. Nashville: Broadman & Holman, 1992.

———. "Why Do We Preach? A Foundation for Christian Preaching, pt. 2." *Commentary.* No pages. Online: http://www.albertmohler.com/commentary_read.php?cdate=2005-12-16.

Mohler, R. Albert, Jr., Daniel L. Akin, and Bruce A. Ware. "Faculty Forum: What Does It Mean to Be an Evangelical?" *The Southern Seminary Magazine (The TIE)* 4 (2001) 4–9.

Moo, Douglas J. *2 Peter and Jude.* NIV Application Commentary. Grand Rapids: Zondervan, 1996.

Muirhead, John Henry. *The Platonic Tradition in Anglo-Saxon Philosophy.* London: Macmillan, 1931.

Newton, William Wilberforce. *Yesterday with the Fathers.* New York: Cochrane, 1910.

O'Brien, Peter T. *Colossians, Philemon.* Word Biblical Commentary, vol. 44. Waco, TX: Word, 1982.

Olford, Stephen R., and David L. Olford. *Anointed Expository Preaching.* Nashville: Broadman & Holman, 1998.

Oliphant, Margaret. *A Memoir of the Life of Principal Tulloch.* London: William Blackwell and Sons, 1889.

Olson, Roger E. *The Story of Christian Theology: Twenty Centuries of Tradition & Reform.* Downers Grove, IL: InterVarsity, 1999.

Packer, J. I. "Authority in Preaching." In *The Gospel in the Modern World,* edited by Martyn Eden and David F. Wells, 198–212. London: Inter-Varsity, 1991.

Pattison, T. Harwood. *The History of Christian Preaching.* Philadelphia: American Baptist Publication Society, 1903.

Perry, William Stevens. *The Episcopate in America.* New York: Christian Literature, 1895.

Piper, John. "The Divine Majesty of the Word: John Calvin, the Man, and His Preaching." *The Southern Baptist Journal of Theology* 2 (1999) 4–15.

———. *The Supremacy of God in Preaching.* Grand Rapids: Baker, 1990.

Politzer, Jerome F. "Theological Ideas in the Preaching of Phillips Brooks." *Historical Magazine of the Protestant Episcopal Church* 2 (1964) 157–59.

Quicke, Michael J. *360-Degree Preaching: Hearing, Speaking, and Living the Word.* Grand Rapids: Baker, 2003.

Quintilian. *Institutio Oratoria.* Translated by H. E. Butler. Loeb Classical Library. Cambridge, MA: Harvard University Press, 1921.

Reid, Robert Stephen. "Postmodernism and the Function of the New Homiletic in Post-Christendom Congregations." *Homiletic* 20 (1995) 1–13.

Reid, Robert, Jeffrey Bullock, and David Fleer. "Preaching as the Creation of an Experience: The Not-So-Rational Revolution of the New Homiletic." *The Journal of Communication and Religion* 18 (1995) 1–9.

Resner, André, Jr. *Preacher and Cross: Person and Message in Theology and Rhetoric.* Grand Rapids: Eerdmans, 1999.

Reymond, Robert L. "Incarnation." In *Evangelical Dictionary of Theology.* Edited by Walter A. Elwell. Grand Rapids: Baker, 1984.

Robertson, F. W. *Sermons: Second Series.* London: Kegan Paul, Trench, and Trubner, 1900.

Robinson, Haddon W. *Biblical Preaching: The Development and Delivery of Expository Messages.* Second edition. Grand Rapids: Baker, 2001.

Sanders, Charles Richard. *Coleridge and the Broad Church Movement.* Durham, NC: Duke University Press, 1942.

Schaff, Philip. *The Creeds of Christendom: With a History and Critical Notes.* Fourth edition. New York: Harper & Brothers, 1919.

Seeley, John Robert. *Ecce Homo: A Survey of the Life and Work of Jesus Christ.* Boston: Roberts Brothers, 1893.

Shaddix, Jim. *The Passion-Driven Sermon: Changing the Way Pastors Preach and Congregations Listen.* Nashville: Broadman & Holman, 2003.

Smart, James. *The Strange Silence of the Bible.* London: SCM, 1966.

Smith, H. Sheldon, editor. *Horace Bushnell.* New York: Oxford University Press, 1965.

Stein, Robert H. *A Basic Guide to Interpreting the Bible: Playing by the Rules.* Grand Rapids: Baker, 1994.

Stott, John R. W. *Between Two Worlds: The Art of Preaching in the Twentieth Century.* Grand Rapids: Eerdmans, 1982.

Strauss, David Friedrich. *Life of Jesus.* Translated by George Elliot. New York: Macmillan, 1892.

Teague, David. "Incarnational Preaching." In *Postmodern Preaching: Exploring How to Preach Christ to Postmodern People.* No pages. Online: http://www.postmodernpreaching.net/incarnational.htm.

Temple, William. *Nature, Man, and God.* London: Macmillan, 1934.

Theological Dictionary of the New Testament. 10 vols. Edited by Gerhard Kittel and Gerhard Friedrich. Translated by G. W. Bromiley. Grand Rapids: Eerdmans, 1964–76.

Thornbury, Gregory Alan. "Prolegomena: Introduction to the Task of Theology." In *A Theology for the Church*, edited by Daniel L. Akin, 2–70. Nashville: B&H, 2007.

Thulin, Richard L. *The "I" of the Sermon: Autobiography in the Pulpit.* Minneapolis: Fortress, 1989.

Thwing, C. F. "Phillips Brooks: His Power and Method as a Preacher." *The Review of Reviews* 7 (1893) 178–79.

Tisdale, Leonora Tubbs. *Preaching as Local Theology and Folk Art.* Minneapolis: Augsburg Fortress, 1997.

Turnbull, Ralph G. *From the Close of the Nineteenth Century to the Middle of the Twentieth Century, and American Preaching during the Seventeenth, Eighteenth, and Nineteenth Centuries.* Vol. 3 of *A History of Preaching.* Grand Rapids: Baker, 1974.

Tyng, Charles R., editor. *Record of the Life and Work of the Rev. Stephen Higginson Tyng, D.D., and History of St. George's Church, New York, to the Close of His Rectorship.* New York: E. P. Dutton, 1890.

Vines, Jerry, and Jim Shaddix. *Power in the Pulpit: How to Prepare and Deliver Expository Sermons.* Chicago: Moody, 1999.

Vinton, Alexander H. *Sermons.* Philadelphia: Herman Hooker, 1856.

Wacker, Grant. "The Holy Spirit and the Spirit of the Age in American Protestantism, 1880–1910." In *Reckoning with the Past: Historical Essays on American Evangelicalism for the Institute for the Study of American Evangelicals*, edited by D. G. Hart, 267–88. Grand Rapids: Baker, 1995.

Warfield, Benjamin B. *The Inspiration and Authority of the Bible.* Reprint, Phillipsburg, NJ: Presbyterian & Reformed, 1948.

Wells, David F. *The Person of Christ: A Biblical and Historical Analysis of the Incarnation.* Westchester, IL: Crossway, 1984.

White, David Lewis. "The Preaching of Phillips Brooks." ThD diss., The Southern Baptist Theological Seminary, 1949.

Wiersbe, Warren W. "Phillips Brooks: A Preacher of Truth and Life." In *Phillips Brooks, The Joy of Preaching*, 9–21. Grand Rapids: Kregel, 1989.

Wilkins, Steve, and Alan G. Padgett. *Faith & Reason in the Nineteenth Century.* Vol. 2 of *Christianity & Western Thought: A History of Philosophers, Ideas, & Movements.* Downers Grove, IL: InterVarsity, 2000.

Willimon, William H. *Proclamation and Theology.* Nashville: Abingdon, 2005.

Woolverton, John F. *The Education of Phillips Brooks.* Chicago: University of Illinois Press, 1995.

York, Hershael W., and Scott A. Blue. "Is Application Necessary in the Expository Sermon?" *The Southern Baptist Journal of Theology* 2 (1999) 70–84.

York, Hershael W., and Bert Decker. *Preaching with Bold Assurance: A Solid and Enduring Approach to Engaging Exposition.* Nashville: Broadman & Holman, 2003.